AF461847

# FEMALE FEAR FACTORY

PUMLA DINEO GQOLA

# FEMALE FEAR FACTORY

## Unravelling Patriarchy's Cultures of Violence

PUMLA DINEO GQOLA

Cassava Republic Press edition 2022
Abuja – London



A CIP catalogue record for this book is available from the National Library of Nigeria and the British Library.

ISBN: 978-1-913175-15-3
eISBN: 978-1-913175-16-0

Cover design: Wendy Scott
Book design: Deepak Sharma (Prepress Plus)

Printed and bound in Great Britain by Clays

Distributed in Nigeria by Yellow Danfo
Distributed worldwide by Ingram Publisher Services International

For Yethu

# CONTENTS

**Preface** ix

**Introduction:** The Genesis of an Idea xiv

**Chapter 1:** Manufacturing Female Fear 1

**Chapter 2:** Fear, Fluency and Control 23

**Chapter 3:** Dangerous Fictions 41

**Chapter 4:** Mythologising Misogyny 53

**Chapter 5:** The False Promise of Safety 67

**Chapter 6:** Femicidal Intimacy 80

**Chapter 7:** Bodies of Knowledge 95

**Chapter 8:** Foreign Familiars 114

**Chapter 9:** Fearing Feminists 131

**Chapter 10:** Safety, Nationalism, and COVID 141

**Departures:** Refusing the Prison of Fear – A Diary 152

**Acknowledgements** 159

**Notes** 160

**Bibliography** 166

# PREFACE

'[S]tories are a major way we make communal, transcendent meaning out of human experience.' – Paula Gunn Allen[1]

As I wrote this book, I had cause to revisit 'In the Clarity of a Third-Class Compartment', from a short story collection edited by Khadija Sesay and Helon Habila. I had written it in my twenties but published the story the following decade. In the piece, the woman narrator and her partner travel in a third-class carriage through Cape Town's Southern Suburbs.

During the journey, he tells her a story about his day, but is oblivious to how distracted she is. Although they sit holding hands and touching shoulders in the physical realm, emotionally they could not be further apart. Because the narrator is a woman and her partner is not, and perhaps because the unfolding drama occurs in the mother tongue he does not share with her, he does not pay attention to the spectacular staging of the Female Fear Factory around them.

Fellow occupants of the carriage include workers returning home at the end of the day, uniformed school children, and a group of young men whose entrance is marked by an ostentatious show of masculinity. As the group members loudly announce their arrival, the mood in the carriage shifts. Older men watch them attentively, while younger women move away as inconspicuously as possible, given the space limitations.

Other passengers feign indifference, burying their faces in books, looking out the window, and willing the group's gaze away from their own bodies. Overestimating their power, the young men misread the scene. They assume that the occupants are primed for an orgy of violent masculinities. It is the kind of society where people look away from eruptions of public violence in the name of 'minding their own business' and staying safe, but this carriage has one too many busybodies.

First, one person challenges the group's loutish behaviour towards the schoolgirls. Then another supports the first. Soon, it is clear that the youth are outnumbered and the travellers are not intimidated by them. The targets of the men's aggression are relieved and freed by the older people's intervention. For the startled posse, the next station cannot come soon enough for them to alight from the train.

The narrator and her partner eventually arrive at their destination, just as he reaches the end of his story about whatever exciting things occupied his day, and this entire trip across town. As they make their way out of the station, the narrator has a second illuminating experience, from which her partner is once again excluded. She does not deliberately exclude him from these encounters, and neither one is engineered by her. She is deeply affected and changed by them. He has not even noticed them.

Having recounted his story, he now turns to her to find out about her day. Her answer is brief and jars with what the reader has just witnessed. She offers a response that suggests that her day was unspectacular.

At readings of this story in the 1990s, the audience would gasp or laugh nervously at her response. There was always recognition. Many in the audience had been in the position of the schoolgirls harassed in my story. In most cases, nobody had intervened.

Until recently, I had not reread this story in twelve years, but I was grateful for the coincidence of another project requiring that I do so as this book was going to press.

Although the 'Female Fear Factory' and the 'manufacture of female fear' were coinages from my 2015 book, *Rape: A South African Nightmare*, the story points to an earlier preoccupation with the ways in which fear and gender intersect in public places. In *Rape*, I sought to understand not only the constructions of rape culture, but also the strategies for interrupting the routine terrorisation of women. I called this form of disrupting patriarchy 'the interruption of the Female Fear Factory.' The rereading of my short story highlighted how the idea had been in formation long before that previous book's inception.

When I wrote the short story, I was living in Cape Town, and the train was one of the means of transport I sometimes used to travel to different parts of the Southern Suburbs, the city centre or Muizenberg. Trains and taxis had a prominence in the short stories I wrote in my twenties.

At that time, short stories were part of what I regularly wrote and would later go on to publish, here and there, in various edited collections. I was already thinking through ideas of how to expand a feminist project that would change what it means to be a woman out and about, in any part of my country and in the world. Trains were particularly interesting to me, both as a mode of travel and for their symbolic potential for transformation when represented in literature. They featured frequently in the work I was analysing for my MA thesis on *Staffrider* literature.

They also made regular appearances in Miriam Tlali's work, which I was reading both inside and outside of *Staffrider* literary magazine. I was reading her work as a pioneering feminist writer who was deeply concerned with the ways in which Blackwomen responded to attempts to silence, humiliate, or kill them in public spaces. The short stories and poems of her peers were littered with the broken bodies of Blackwomen as the tablets on which lessons about proper behaviour were inscribed. Tlali was one of a handful of writers who wrote against this tradition.

So, perhaps I owe a significant amount of my thinking about the organisation of public space in specifically gendered ways to the way in which that feminist, whose work has been very important to me, positioned her women characters in various spaces, including trains and other modes of transport. It is clear that hers is a project that is uninterested in the staging of victimisation, and there are many instances of delightful, disruptive solidarity among women characters. Instead of a slew of victims, her women characters are written in such a way that even when faced with the most brutal of circumstances, they offer a transformative vision of feminist imagination.

And perhaps it was because her stories amplified the small daily acts of defiance that were part of my own and other women's lives, that this story took the shape it did. Tlali's protagonists escape patriarchal violence through very different registers, so my work was not a replication of hers. However, it clearly was in conversation with her oeuvre. I wanted to fantasise about ending sexual harassment not just through protest, but through the refusal of ordinary people to comply with patriarchal power. The specific fantasy became the short story.

Rather than map my short story, Tlali's writings, and my 2015 book chronologically, I embrace the recurring narrative, revisiting the idea of patriarchal threat and feminist imaginative resistance. At the time of writing the short story, I had already been a feminist activist as an undergraduate student, had recently trained as a rape crisis counsellor (where I still volunteered twice a week), went clubbing every weekend, and was consciously building a career as a future feminist professor and author.

In 2015, as I wrote my third book, I was a feminist professor, still involved in feminist activist work outside the academy, and deeply disillusioned with the South African left. The story of the book *Female Fear Factory* is therefore not a linear one.

In her editor's introduction to *Spider Woman's Granddaughters*, Native American feminist author and professor Paula Gunn Allen reminds us that, as defiant women, we write both out of and into traditions. She also underscores the ways in which both oppressive and liberatory registers construct stories.

By story, I mean both what we recognise as a specific kind of narrative, as well as the less obvious tales through which violent, hierarchical power hides violence for purposes of domination. Some narratives present themselves clearly as such. Patriarchy relies heavily on the symbolic; on the arrangement of certain events as though they are not constructed, as though their internal organisational logic is natural, automatic, and inevitable.

In contrast, I use feminist accounts to poke holes in this façade of inevitability, by laying bare the lies at the heart of oppressive, intersecting systems, and amplifying the possibilities for imagining freedom. The recital of women's continuous defiance, feminist resistance and multigenerational claims to freedom matter as much more than mere examples.

Patriarchy is brutal. It is normalised in public and private spaces. It deploys entire institutions explicitly and through deception. As a key feminist principle, therefore, I write against the Female Fear Factory in defamiliarising and energising ways. As such, I never just portray patriarchy's brutality at work without gesturing towards its unmaking. We must never leave patriarchy uncommented on as we illustrate its workings. This principle informs how most of my chapters are written: illustrations of the differing dimensions of the Female Fear Factory are juxtaposed with stories of defiance and feminist courage. It is never enough to simply illustrate how patriarchy works in order to understand it. The feminist imperative is to think against it, strategise against it, and consistently work to destroy it. The feminist articulations in each chapter are not romanticised as victory. But they always matter because they create something: sometimes illumination, and at other times strategies for the smashing of patriarchy. It may be a long, bloody battle, but I am committed to the consistent creation of feminist hope and a patriarchy-free future.

# INTRODUCTION:
## The Genesis of an Idea

'Female Fear Factory' is a formulation from one of my previous books, *Rape: A South African Nightmare*. I had coined the term there as one of my explanations for how rape as a patriarchal tool became so commonplace. I had focused on South Africa, partly because this is where I live, and partly because it is the location for the bulk of my anti-rape work. I understood that many of the dimensions of rape I outlined and analysed in that book, as well as the strategies I developed to interrupt rape culture, were applicable to patriarchal societies elsewhere.

When I wrote *Rape,* I focused exclusively on rape and how it has historically been set up and propped up as a language. Rape is an expression of patriarchal violence, and one that is enabled by the Female Fear Factory. In turn, rape culture contributes to sustaining fear.

I understood then, as I do now, that history is always much more than context and/or background. I wanted to zoom in on specific eras to illustrate the ways in which certain institutions were implicated in how South Africa experiences and responds to rape.

When we understand the roles of institutions in building rape culture, giving it legitimacy, we temper our expectations that these same institutions will offer a way out of the very same system of violence they have helped to shape. In many places around the world, the police and courts are called 'the legal justice system' and/or 'the criminal justice system.' This may have a particular history, but this naming hides the differences between legal justice requirements and the use of justice to refer to fairness. Consequently, many people – including activists engaged in struggles for a fair, equal world – expect justice and fairness from legal offices.

They do so, fully aware of how the law is implicated in legitimising inequality, and they do so often in recognition of the urgency of creating feminist jurisprudence. After all, slavery and indenture were once legal practices, as was apartheid, which underscores the importance of its declaration as a crime against humanity.

The wage gap continues to be legal. In other words, despite the fact that law has historically created – not just enabled – inequality and injustice, many turn to the police and courts, and are disappointed when these offices and institutions do not deliver fairness. Far from being naïve expectations, these are legitimate demands for recognition, and the overhaul of the existing systems through which justice can be attained. The law is a powerful mapping and regulatory system that cannot be left in the hands of what US feminist theorist bell hooks calls 'white supremacist capitalist patriarchy.'

Concerned with how deeply embedded rape culture was in these systems, I specifically used certain examples that trace the roots of the current South African legal system to a slavocratic past, and later, the colonial order that enabled the routine rape of enslaved and other Blackwomen as a matter of course – while at the same time refusing to officially recognise such rape as rape. Slowly, as the rape of Blackwomen became institutionalised, normalised and mythologised, these women were constructed as 'unrapeable.' To be unrapeable does not mean 'to be impossible to rape.' It means the opposite. The unrapeable is that category of humans constructed and marked as free to be raped without consequence. Blackwomen are constructed as unrapeable through the marking of their bodies as available for rape as enslaved women, and partly through the refusal of the court system to ever convict a man for the rape of a slave woman throughout the era of slavery in the Cape.

Second, layered onto what I have just outlined, is the cruel mythologising of the slave prison as the Cape's 'first brothel,' obscuring the fact that both Dutch and English men participated in the large-scale permitted rape of those enslaved women who had escaped and then been recaptured, the women captured and awaiting sale, and other enslaved women being held at the Cape Lodge. To call it a brothel imputes agency, choice, and compensation – however limited – to those women who held the legal status of mere objects and were therefore unable to either consent or resist.

Third, during colonial warfare, British soldiers routinely celebrated wins in battle by raping 'native women,' effectively cementing the relationship between warfare and large-scale rape, and normalising rape as part of warfare. Importantly, while the pairing of rape and warfare has a long history in Western Europe, this phenomenon was introduced to southern Africa (and possibly beyond) through colonialism. In other words, while rape predated colonialism because rape is a necessary part of all patriarchal societies, southern African men did not rape women of the vanquished army as part of the business of warfare and celebrating their victories. Indeed, the fact that they did not rape white women and kill white children when they won colonial battles and wars caused extensive confusion for the British. Ultimately, this was seen as further evidence of unsophisticated native masculinity.

The construction of Blackwomen as unrapeable becomes an important stage in the creation of permissible forms of violence, and the impossibility of justice, since the rape itself is not recognised as harm. Is it reasonable, then, to expect a criminal justice system built partly on establishing permission to Blackwomen's bodies to provide justice for Blackwomen who have been raped? The question is deceptively simple. The contemporary South African legal justice system routinely fails to offer justice for women, especially Blackwomen, who report cases of rape and other forms of gender-based violence. The relationship I trace in *Rape* is more than causal; it is linked to a question I ask later in this book, *Female Fear Factory*, about the relationships that exist between institutions and violence.

As a former student feminist activist, and then, for over two decades, as someone who teaches at university, I am keenly aware of the ways in which sexual violence continues to be an enduring aspect of university life across the globe, while university policies to deal with sexual violence and gender-based harm in their various iterations abound. I wanted to know exactly how rape culture was constructed historically, to understand the specific role fear played in this, as well as what opportunities exist for feminist intervention, once we better understand the intersections of rape and fear.

In this book, *Female Fear Factory*, I examine the deeply embedded sexual violence that is part of university institutional culture and foundational history. In *Rape*, only one chapter is dedicated to the place of fear in the construction of patriarchal violence. I called that particular chapter 'The Female Fear Factory.' In the intervening six years, my thinking on the Female Fear Factory has shifted considerably, as I spent more time thinking about it.

## What is the 'Female Fear Factory' in that previous book chapter?

It is a theatrical and public performance of patriarchal policing of and violence towards women and others cast as female, who are, therefore, considered safe to violate. It requires an audience, and relies on a series of recognisable cues to communicate with those who watch, because patriarchy ensures that we are socialised to recognise these cues in a process of fluency on which I expand in this book, in the chapter titled 'Fear, Fluency, and Control.' The Female Fear Factory travels through respectability and through shame, and is normalised through repetition so that we no longer recognise it for what it is, consequently taking it for granted as 'life.' I argued in my first coinage that questioning it is urgent, as is interrupting it and making it strange. Rendering it 'strange' can also be how we make the Female Fear Factory unnatural and ultimately how we take it apart, to create new ways of living.

The Female Fear Factory threatens women, mostly to remind us that nothing belongs to us – not even our bodies, neither in private nor public spaces. Its spectacular aspect is important because it communicates both to the target and to the audience the possibility of being the victim, and teaches and enshrines power in patriarchal society.

As a system of production, it relies on several aspects to be able to work, including the recognition of people as falling into categories of female (and therefore safe to violate), as well as the recognition of the safety of the aggressor. The relationship between sex as coded in our chromosomes and the status of women, gender, and sexual minorities as female, is not an automatic one. Nor is it merely a biological slippage, as I show in the first chapter.

In chapter 1, 'Manufacturing Female Fear,' I demonstrate how women are rendered as socially female, and therefore safe to violate. Women are not automatically female, but are made so, in a process that leads to different genders being *made* female.

To be socialised as female makes women, and sometimes other sexually minoritised people, safe to be subjected to the Female Fear Factory. Fluency in fear – and making us police ourselves – is how women are kept in check. It also sometimes works to remind some men and transgender people that they are like women – because they too can be made female – and are therefore not just rapeable, as originally conceived, but also generally safe to target for different types of patriarchal violence.

Since that first coinage, I have had time to fine-tune aspects of the Female Fear Factory and to think of it in relation to patriarchy and patriarchal violence of different forms. I extend the definition of the Female Fear Factory in the 'Manufacturing Female Fear' chapter, and extend conceptions of how fluency is achieved in the chapter that follows. From chapter 3 onwards, I pay attention to varied sites of the Female Fear Factory, not to offer a conclusive and definitive cartography, but to show the ways in which it can express itself under the banners of institutionality, femicide, xenophobic Afrophobia, different forms of anti-feminist backlash, and the mythologisation of women as victims of violence.

As a feminist, I am as interested in the strategies adopted – and made possible – to make the Female Fear Factory visible, as I am in understanding it. Consequently, I interrogate various imaginative, courageous feminist energies put to this use from distinctly different societies across the globe. When the Chilean feminist collective Las Tesis composed 'Un Violador en Tu Camino' (A Rapist in Your Path), the accusation that 'El Violador Eres Tu' ('The Rapist is You') was directed at everyday rapists as well as institutional rapists: the police that routinely use sexual and other forms of violence, the courts, universities and many other sites which provide cover for sexual violators. It resonated with women across the world and quickly went viral beyond Chilean and other Latin American cities. This recognition of the entanglements of individual rape acts enabled and protected by patriarchy, on the one hand, with institutional brutality on the other, illuminates both micro and macro dimensions of patriarchal violence. Many of the lessons we learn from studying and agitating against rape apply to other aspects of patriarchal domination, as evidenced in Las Tesis' viral anthem that speaks of institutionalised patriarchy broadly – naming rape, femicide, the judiciary, political leadership, and police forces as violators.

Put differently, we can do anti-rape work because we understand how patriarchy works, but anti-rape work further illuminates patriarchy in aspects unconcerned with rape. In *Rape*, I use the phrases 'Female Fear Factory' and 'the manufacture of female fear' interchangeably. I recognised as I did so that by the dawn of the twenty-first century, there had been significant shifts in the various meanings of the word 'manufacture,' which, on the one hand, attach to specific conditions of capitalist production. On the other hand, I was also referring back to the use of the word to gesture towards forms of making through synthesis – putting things together – that predate the conveyor-belt-type factory process. I wanted to highlight its social production through evoking this older meaning of 'made by human hand,' to signal 'made through human agency.' This is productive tension because, while the Female Fear Factory has become a critical aspect of post-industrial revolution life, its roots lie in older forms of patriarchy.

Put differently, it is important to simultaneously keep in mind the ways in which fear has a 'factory,' and the ways in which it predates and exceeds this type of production. To use both these phrases, then, is how I keep both the ancient traces of fear and its mutating capitalist, globalised articulations in view.

Both phrases refer to the spectacular staging of a product (fear) that is key to the control of women. Female fear (the product), and its production (the factory) are necessary for patriarchal control. Fear is fostered through exaggerated visual performance, audible cues, and other coded signs, all of which are repeated until the target audiences have mastered the form of communication and have started to take fear for granted, as something that is inevitable. This fear colours decisions made about movement, aspiration, desire, and other aspects of life in an automatic manner once fluency is achieved. In other words, fluency in the registers of the Female Fear Factory shapes areas of life that appear unlinked to violence and control.

It made sense to use the language of manufacture and factories, because female fear works like other, easily recognisable systems of production that are found everywhere in capitalist economies. The Female Fear Factory works like a real-life factory in its rationale, its processes, as well as its position within the realm of the public, as I show below.

Like a real factory, it takes up unapologetic public space, even if its products readily travel across the boundaries of public/private realms. The Female Fear Factory's publicness is not accidental. This very publicness is vital to its successful operation. Substantial bodies of work by feminists in the twentieth century have taught us the ways in which patriarchal societies traditionally divide the worlds of women from those of men through an oppositional private versus public split. In this division, public space becomes the domain of 'the masculine' and men, as well as the location of valued political-economic labour, in the first instance. Thus, even in those societies which boast a previous, long history of women as political and economic leaders, both the 'captains of industry' and most of those in high political office are men. Even in democracies such as Rwanda and Sweden, which have the largest number of women in high political office, the idea of the public as being 'the terrain of men' is evident. This is so despite diverse historic traditions of divisions of labour in many societies, and directly because of the history of world formation over the last three hundred years.

But what does it mean to speak about the Female Fear Factory as public, in a context within which definitions of publicness abound? By public, here, I intend two meanings. First, I refer to what Alubo defines as:

> geo-territorial space occupied by a country or its political divisions into provinces, regions or states. The public space is also used to refer to physical places such as parks, gardens and shopping malls which are open to the public. It also includes work-related spaces such as factory sites and bureaucracies.[2]

This first sense of public then is the visible, largely political and economic realm, coupled with some areas of formal recreational and flexible use. In this first sense, along with the park, I intend the pavement, the street and all other places in which the possibility of coming into contact with others cannot be entirely predicted.

The second meaning of public is 'the public sphere,' which is less a geo-spatial conception, and more a contested space of engagement. Ideally, the public sphere refers to a discursive terrain, in which all can participate democratically in the germination and development of the collective consciousness of the time.

In what follows, I spend some time illustrating how the Female Fear Factory is public, and why it needs to be public to work.

## Fear and Confinement

A range of examples illuminate how the Female Fear Factory is public in the first sense. In Saudi Arabia, although there are reportedly over ten million women who form part of that country's general populace, until 2018 there were laws against women driving in that country. Despite significant increases in the number of women entering the labour force, and specifically high office in political and military posts, this unevenness tells us something about that country's understanding of the relationships between public space entitlements and gender.

To have a law that criminalises women's ability to move freely in public space highlights the legitimised punishment for women staking claims over the public, and their actions within that realm. Freedom of movement is the articulation of ownership of public space. To legislate against something – in this case, women driving – is to offer a threat that can be met with force. Over many years, the women who petitioned monarchs (beginning with King Abdullah in the last decade of the twentieth century); the ones who drove and faced not just arrest but the confiscation of their passports; the ones who waged international media campaigns; the activists sentenced to lashings; and the ones who were kept in jail even after the law had been changed all form part of the defiance and enactment of the Female Fear Factory. These activists were fluent in the Female Fear Factory. More than this, however, they refused to be bound by its rules.

When a state uses the threat of force to stop women driving, it communicates clearly, through the threat of bodily harm, not just that women are excluded from the definition of public (ownership), but also that any attempt to contest this exclusion will be met with violence. Confinement is the most consistently applied form of legal punishment, as is exclusion from public participation. Confinement is understood to be both oppressive and universally legal.

Here, the enforced dependency created by the ban on women driving, and the imprisonment of women who defied the law by choosing to drive, are two sides of the same coin. Women can be frightened out of engaging in certain activities and occupying public space; this fear is heightened by the threat of legal consequences from the state's actors: police, legislators, and courts. In a world where criminal courts and policing are named 'the justice system,' it is easy to confuse the law for the terrain of fairness (justice). However, laws regulate what is legitimate activity in a society, and here, in public. The banning of women's driving and the imprisonment of women who defy this unjust set of laws legitimise keeping women confined. They are articulations of the same connections between publicness and fear. The additional confiscation of the protesting women's passports forms a further layer of entrapment. Not only can these women not drive in their country, but they may also not opt out of such a society by moving to a country with rules different from their own. Their deliberate entrapment is emphasised by this additional layer of control.

The threatening message is clear to these specific women, and to those who are their potential allies, supporters, and peer protestors. This threat and the accompanying punishment is not performed privately. Indeed, the punishment is the reinforcement of the threat. Spectators can see that the law has teeth. It is theatrical, spectacular, and forceful. Furthermore, that women activists were kept in detention after their victory in achieving legislative change is reinforcement of the manufacture of female fear, because even when women win substantial victories, they are not safe. Aziza al-Yousef, Loujain al-Hathloul, Eman al-Nafjan, Aisha Almane, and Madeha al-Ajroush were all kept in detention, uncharged, for more than a hundred days after the ban was lifted. What is more, a year after their detention, al-Nafjan was barred by her country from travelling to accept an international award. These feminists reported that the kinds of violence meted out against them in their extended detention included sexual assault. Sexual assault is routinely used by states to discipline women activists, as it is used to discipline all women everywhere. In detention, sexual assault reminds women of their legitimate place: powerless and weak. This is a particularly important lesson for those women who have exercised their power to claim the freedom to push against the boundaries of patriarchal states. Sexual violence is yet another attempt to break troublesome women down, make them smaller, make them female through violence and shame.

However, feminists understand this, as do many other troublesome women, however they identify. Sexual violence is war against women for being women, but it is enacted individually, to isolate the victim and remake her through violence and shame. When these same women name sexual violence as part of the state's brutal toolkit, they again exceed the categories into which the state-sanctioned violations try to lock them. They feel the effects of violence, but refuse the definitional power of this violence by publicly naming and refusing shame. In this regard, their experience mirrors the experiences of women in detention across many parts of the world under different regimes.

The example of the experiences of Saudi feminists engaged in a three-decade struggle for the right to drive stages the manufacture of female fear spectacularly. While I refer specifically to a particular stage in Saudi women's struggle for freedom, I recognise that the struggle against driving restrictions occupies the same continuum as the struggle to vote in their past, and the struggle for full recognition of their humanity. For watching women, the threat of imprisonment, sexual assault, public shaming, and prevention from leaving the persecution by fleeing to another country all communicate clearly the dangers that will befall wilful women.

Public spaces are not theirs, and any confusion will be met with such virulent force that even victories will not guarantee their safety. Women being punished for illegitimately entering the realm of men must be repeatedly reminded, made to feel out of place through pain. They must also be imagined as conceptually out of place.

However, the multi-generational movement of women activists continues to mobilise for further freedoms, refusing to be pushed back into seclusion, their rightful place under patriarchy.

Feminism is the constant refusal to be held down; it is the fight against being kept in feminine place by the Female Fear Factory, in Saudi Arabia or anywhere else in the world.

Since examples can sometimes crystallise something about a specific society, I now turn to offer another example, from a very different society, and one which is closer to home. Examples work to illustrate, but one example can speak so definitively that people get lost in the detail. For this reason, throughout this book, I will use examples from very different societies to highlight dimensions of the Female Fear Factory. Wherever possible, I will choose examples that do not immediately lend themselves to easy comparison. It is too easy otherwise to make the mistake that many feminists from dominant countries make, of assuming that patriarchy is worse in 'Muslim' or 'Asian,' 'African' or 'Latin American' contexts, when the exact same abuse of power is in clear view in their own societies once they begin to look deeper. When feminists, wherever located, allow ourselves to be pulled into the obfuscations of 'better' or 'worse' patriarchy, we are distracted from the fact of patriarchy's ubiquity. There is no better or worse patriarchy, only patriarchal obfuscation.

My next example of how the Fear Factory works in public ways is from a society where women drivers are a taken-for-granted reality. Post-apartheid South Africa has some of the best protofeminist legislation and political representations in the world.

It would be easy, if we pay attention only to legislation and whose bodies move about in public, to miss the connecting ways in which the Female Fear Factory operates here as it does in Saudi Arabia.

In 2017, while the aforementioned Saudi feminists were fighting against the confinement of women and the legal regulation of women's movement, one of my students invoked the Female Fear Factory in a class discussion that morning when she declared, 'By the time I arrive for this class, at 9am, I have already fought a hundred wars.'

This was a Blackwoman born post-apartheid, a student at the prestigious University of the Witwatersrand in Johannesburg, where I was a full professor at the time. It was a literature class discussion on a topic I no longer recall.

When I invited her to expand on this statement, she articulated her multiple encounters with the Female Fear Factory. Walking from her parents' home to take a minibus taxi, several men had commented on her body and tried to get her attention in a manner that suggested sexual interest, but really communicated entitlement to her body and her exclusion from ownership of public space.

More recently, Koketso Moeti wrote in a column for *Mail & Guardian* about how both verified data and straw polls show the pervasive nature of fear felt by women in public:

> In a popular Twitter thread, a social researcher informally ran a poll asking people to share what they do to avoid being sexually assaulted. All the men responded with different versions of 'nothing,' whereas women listed very specific actions they take daily, such as holding keys as potential weapons and feeling uncomfortable when strapping children into the car seat.
>
> What should be ordinary tasks in adult life, such as getting repairs done or having something installed, easily become very complicated because of the risk that goes with it if you are a woman.

Moeti's words underscore the centrality of fear in women's daily lives. The women who responded to the poll surface the way fear shapes even mundane decisions in their lives, and the ways they have to proceed with the assumption that they will encounter some form of harassment. The stark contrast with the men who responded to the poll points to the manner in which fear operates differently in the lives of men and women.

It is not that patriarchy does not brutalise men, merely that it terrorises women all the time, and the Female Fear Factory is woven into the very fabric of women's lives, because women are always in the process of being made and kept female. Many women also constantly exceed this category. Those of us who are feminists deliberately escape and break parts of patriarchy.

Patriarchy may be hard work for all people, but as feminists we are determined to wear patriarchy out. Street sexual harassment often pretends to be appreciative and complimentary, but its targets see through this lie and understand the intrusion and menacing effects of forced attention. It communicates clearly that they are not free to walk about in public, that they are not safe. Indeed, to step out into the public space between her home and her university requires that my student prepare herself daily to walk through threats in ways best suited to keep her body unharmed. This steeling of the self is recognition that there are no guarantees of safety. It is daily confrontation with and defiance of the Female Fear Factory. In her *Sexual Harassment of Working Women: A Case of Sex Discrimination*, Catharine MacKinnon long ago called this violence presenting as sexual play 'eroticisation of women's subordination.' The author was writing about workplace sexual harassment, but it works here too. In that same book, she also suggests that 'inequality is built into the social conception of female sexuality, of masculinity and femininity, of sexiness and heterosexual attractiveness'[3] in one of many important questions asked in that study.

In South Africa, when we routinely speak in anger against street sexual harassment, we are told that it is the performance of desire and appreciation; we are reminded of older times where this public approach by men was the African equivalent of 'courting' in previous centuries in Europe. This reminder is patriarchal correction. It is an attempt to read against ourselves, be complicit in the eroticisation of our domination. It is not a coincidence that African women are corrected through recourse to ideas of an old Africa that we are all raised to feel nostalgic for. This is violence too, because it places women outside this definition of an old African way of flirting or public exchange.

In addition to being corrective, however, it is also opportunistic and farcical. Women can be harassed and still flirt elsewhere every day. We know the difference between violence and a respectful, playful approach, and since we are not raised in a parallel universe, the men of our societies know the difference too.

My student related to us that eventually reaching the taxi rank and catching the minibus taxi comes with an additional expression of the manufacture of female fear, not relief from it. Upon entering the taxi that morning, she had experienced anxiety about her failure to jot down the vehicle's registration.

For several weeks, there had been news reports of a serial rapist taxi driver who continued to elude arrest, with no identikit circulated to assist the public in his apprehension. This serial rapist targeted women on Oxford Street in the Parktown area, not far from two university campuses situated in Braamfontein – the University of the Witwatersrand and the Auckland Park campus of the University of Johannesburg. Because several taxi routes intersect on Oxford Street, neither the driver's taxi route nor his taxi association were clear from the circulating news reports.

These news reports, coupled with the lack of clarity about the taxi route affected, meant that many women who rely on public transport felt obliged to be extra vigilant. It is important to pause here to imagine what 'extra vigilance' means for women who already always occupy public space with an underlying consciousness of their own unsafety. It also bears noting that while we were all preoccupied with the minibus-taxi-driver-rapist that particular month, we are actually always preoccupied with some version of male violence. Some weeks, we have a specific predator on the loose that has made headlines, and others we do not. However, being constantly bombarded with this kind of information means that vigilance is a permanent state of being for South African women. The Female Fear Factory is relentless.

The young woman in my class then detailed how further self-awareness gripped her as she briskly walked to campus from the taxi drop-off point. This awareness articulated itself as simultaneous knowledge that she could be robbed and/or groped as she made her way to campus across a few blocks in the Johannesburg Central Business District (CBD) and Braamfontein. In other words, she had to walk through fear of 'ordinary' crime as well as fear of assaults on her person, which would not be considered 'crimes.'

The wars my student has waged in self-defence by the time she arrives for her first class at a prestigious institution are not left at the entrance to campus once she has swiped her way in and taken her place in a comfortable air-conditioned room for intellectual pursuit. Her arrival, participation, and excelling in this class are always coloured by this experience of being terrorised. Like the Saudi women who took to driving in defiance, she has to make this trip fully aware of its dangers, refusing the containment that is offered as the alternative. I will say nothing here of the violence that characterises university campuses too. In a later chapter, 'Bodies of Knowledge,' I use the brilliant strategies of other young African women at Nigerian campuses to speak to campus violence and the Female Fear Factory.

It fills me with rage to imagine what we lose as a society – and as a world – when women are forced to excel under these conditions. What more could women like these offer us in the way of excellence if they were free to fully apply themselves under conditions of safety? Who else could we all be if we did not have to surrender a part of our brains to the ever-present fear that persists even when we make a lifelong commitment to dismantle the Female Fear Factory, sometimes brick by brick, and at other times by blowing parts of it up?

Jessica Horn's words on the body as a key site of contestation are particularly instructive here, with very clear connections between the South African woman whose very movement through her city is met with constant commentary, and all the Saudi women imprisoned through various regimes. Horn's words also link forward to the example of 'Schumacher,' the bisexual soap opera character discussed in the next chapter. In her essay, 'Re-righting the Sexual Body,' Horn writes:

> Our bodies are our primary means of participating socially, economically, politically, spiritually and creatively in society. They are the beginning point of the application of rights; the place in which rights are exercised, and for women in particular, the place where rights are most often violated.[4]

The body is the primary avenue for the control, as well as the vehicle used to escape and resist in all three examples. Schumacher, like the iconic champion race driver he renames himself after, flees the physical site of his dehumanisation. More than that, however, through hard work economically, emotionally, and socially, he creates a rewarding, free life for himself. He remakes himself and insists on an affirming life. The Saudi feminists recognise that their confinement is enforced partly through the control of their bodies. They make the connections between movement and freedom that are evident to all those in bondage. When they choose to drive, their bodies are the battleground over which freedom is fought for and won. In Horn's terms, they are unapologetic in the assertion of what should be their rights. In a similar vein, the Wits student may walk through tumultuous terrain as threats are made both directly and indirectly; through comments on her body, and through her heightened awareness of what happens regularly to those who are embodied in a similar fashion. Yet, she must walk as an exercise of a right that is guaranteed to her on paper, but that requires daily assertion and claiming.

In South Africa, there are no cultures of long-term confinement of women into the domestic sphere. Even the most violent patriarchs who make obscene jokes about women's driving do not oppose women's driving *per se*. They are simply demonstrating the general contempt they have for all women for existing – ingrained misogyny. The men from different generations who comment on my student's body do not argue that women should be kept out of view; they simply feel entitled to comment on their appearance. Masculine entitlement of this sort is not just about the assumed right to (voice) an opinion, however. It is also about the assumption that they have a right to women entertaining all men's opinions and responding in ways that show due deflection to them. Put differently, what these men enact is menacing, because socialisation into patriarchal masculinity has taught them that women have an obligation to treat men's words and thoughts as both legitimate and important, especially when expressed in public.

In 'The Meaning of Spatial Boundaries,' Fatema Mernissi teaches us that

> [t]he institutionalized boundaries dividing the parts of society express the recognition of power in one part at the expense of the other. Any transgression of the boundaries is a danger to the social order because it is an attack on the acknowledged allocation of power. The link between boundaries and power is particularly salient in society's sexual patterns.[5]

The ownership of public space is a male right in a very direct sense when women must rely on men for certain kinds of mobility beyond a short distance. To be allowed to drive as a woman and, moreover, to politically organise for the right to do so when denied this right – and then to win, is to thoroughly attack 'the acknowledged allocation of power' by claiming some of that power for women, and refusing to defer to the institutionalised power of men over women and all public space. For my student to make her way across the city to attend classes constantly troubles the unsaid – but nonetheless clear – boundaries about public space. It is not accidental either that the threats of violence are sexualised in her case.

These men know that the oft-posited excuse that such commentary is playful, appreciative banter is a lie. This is why they refuse to offer the same kind of complimentary attention to other strange men in the same spaces. It is also why they are so quick to defend the women they love – mothers, daughters, friends, and sisters – from the same attention. The young woman in my class was fluent in the Female Fear Factory's regulation of public space – before, during, and after the minibus taxi trip. She had acquired this fluency over nearly two decades of being a girl and a woman in a society with routine street sexual harassment.

She was also determined to defy it in the streets – and wherever else it sought to flatten her. On the face of it, these South African and Saudi Arabian feminists appear to live in societies organised along very different relationships to the patriarchal policing of women's bodies in public. Yet, the Female Fear Factory communicates to women like my student and the Saudi driving women in very similar registers. The Female Fear Factory's publicness in this manner can co-exist with increasing statistics of women entering careers and leadership roles in public life. It does not simply melt away when challenged but needs consistent defiance.

Here, I choose examples of women who feel the threat and nonetheless go out in public, because defiance of the Female Fear Factory is the only way we can chip away at it and ultimately blow it up. There is an additional investment in choosing examples of women who feel the fear and go out anyway: to illustrate that it requires courage to live as a woman in a patriarchal society; yet, courage does not, and indeed cannot, depend on fearlessness. (While women of all political persuasions brave the public daily in South Africa, the student whose story I choose here does self-identify as a feminist.)

These examples demonstrate one way in which the Female Fear Factory is public in a physical, geo-spatial sense. The second sense of public I wish to invoke is what has often been called the public sphere, or arena, after Jürgen Habermas's formulation, which was later problematised through the surfacing of gendered and classed power in the now equally canonical work of Nancy Fraser and others. The Habermasian public sphere may have emerged from public discussions in places like squares and coffee shops. However, it refers to something more abstract.

The public sphere is less physical and more conceptual. It is the public space of ideas, the general understanding of how things and specific relations work, the valuation logics, and the terms through which meaning can be made and unmade.

Public spheres are public because they are collectively owned worlds of ideas. In theory, everybody has access to the making and unmaking of a collective consciousness, or an awareness of the guiding ideas of the time, akin to what Raymond Williams long ago termed 'structures of feeling.' This is Habermas' notion, presented as descriptive, but shown by Fraser and subsequent feminists to be both uncritically masculinist and aspirational.

Fraser showed that rather than being truly democratically and publicly constituted, Habermas' public sphere had significant gendered and class dimensions beyond those he makes explicit reference to. Like Fraser, I think the distinctions between 'public' in relation to the state and economy, on the one hand, and 'public sphere,' on the other hand, are very important to retain, rather than collapse. In my earlier examples, I refer to how the Female Fear Factory is enacted through collusion of state and physical spatial regulation – but also in times where legislation and patriarchal spatial regulation appear to pull in different directions. The Female Fear Factory can be a project of the state, but it need not be exclusively so. To this end, I find Zine Magubane's insistence that we think about ideology as inherently contradictory – rather than seamless – useful.

This is how it is possible in both societies used as examples to have the simultaneous embrace of the ideals of 'women's empowerment' in the public sphere, and the circulation of pervasive practices that place women under surveillance. Women's advancement can be seen in the increasing movement of women into professions, including the military, while confinement is enacted by the state. The boundaries may appear blurry, but transgressing them is met with very clear consequential violence.

The public sphere is the fluid, contested realm in which consensus is sometimes reached about the 'common sense,' through a shifting and shiftable agreement. Thinking on the public sphere has advanced to embrace the existence of counterpublics. Viewed as 'an institutionalized arena of discursive interaction,' Fraser nonetheless insists that the Habermasian conception of the public sphere needs considerable work to meaningfully 'yield a category capable of theorising' current relations between counterpublics and the inherent contestation. The public sphere is not an unchanging bourgeois structure but one that is permeable enough for shifts in ideas in directions both transformative and conservative, and for co-existence with these counterpublics.

Indeed, as Fraser herself reminds us in her highly influential essay, 'Rethinking the Public Sphere': 'It is the idea of the public sphere that provides the conceptual condition of possibility for the revisionist critique of its imperfect realization.'[6] Both definitions of what is public illustrate something very important about how the Female Fear Factory exists. There is no automatic, objective reason why the public – in the geo-territorial spatial sense – should be male space. Nor do ideas about how to read and treat women in varying public activities and roles stem from inevitability. This is especially the case when we accept that in most countries, women outnumber men. Even where there are equal numbers of people of all genders, the only reason public space has become synonymous with men's space is due to historical developments of patriarchal power across the globe. This historical trajectory has also marked the public space as where substantial, valuable work occurs, because this is where visible, valued work and activity occur in late capitalist patriarchies. Therefore 'formal work' is located in the realm of the public and the most devalued work is kept largely out of public view.

In the quotation above, Alubo mentions both parks (the recreational) and factories or offices as public. The public has clear rules, and it is also visible. The Female Fear Factory works like a real factory in its logic and relationship to publicness. Like a factory that produces physical products, it takes up space. And although we work with seemingly commonsensical ideas about public space as collectively owned by all of us, another meaning of a collective is a 'public'.

Factories show the asymmetrical relationships between space and ownership, or power. Factories occupy public space, yet even collectively administered production lines work on lines of distinction when it comes to ownership. They may be owned by a group, say, in a publicly listed company. However, they do not belong to everybody in that society in the same way. Nor do all members of the public enjoy the same benefits or relationships of proximity to collectively owned factories and factory processes. The seemingly commonsensical understanding of public space as shared, collectively owned space nonetheless continues to clash significantly with power as played out in public. This means women – and all other oppressed in any space – walk around with something akin to Du Bois's double consciousness, and therefore multiple senses of truth. For women to survive and live, we have to proceed as though we believe public spaces are ours too – in literal and symbolic ways. They do belong to us, and they do not. At the same time, messages passed on through the pervasive preoccupation with our unsafety communicate clearly that public spaces belong to men. To make women feel out of place in public is how public spaces are ring-fenced in patriarchy. Street harassment, restrictions on women driving, and the many other tools of the Female Fear Factory are how public space is taken away from women. Continuing to take up space is how we claim space as belonging to all of us.

The Female Fear Factory takes up publicness as a performance of legitimacy, since it is visible to all to witness. Spectators are affected by it in one way or another – either recognising it, to later perform in similar ways, or understanding the threat in the performance of who can be harmed in public.

In societies where public sexual harassment is acceptable, women and gender-fluid people learn early that when they are attacked and/or belittled in public, others will look away.

They learn just as quickly that the best way to avoid the escalation of this violence – which, again, is unlikely to be stopped by those witnessing it – is to pretend that it is not happening. We are taught over a lifetime that the only way to remain safe is to look away, that it is dangerous to defend ourselves.

The publicness of the performance of these threats – in other words the public production of fear – marks public space as belonging to those who perform ownership over others. The repetition is authorised and sets up a series of certainties: that the harassed will retreat and the harasser will remain unchallenged.

Those who witness it learn from the inaction of all others. Inaction and deflection become the normalised response to the Female Fear Factory. That which occurs repeatedly without question becomes the norm. Once normalised, it is harder to question recurrence, until there have been so many instances that it ceases to be seen. However, when we refuse to keep quiet when trivialisation happens in front of us in public, we make more cracks in patriarchy's manufacture of female fear. We create a new normal. Therefore, some of this work must be done in small, everyday public acts, repeatedly.

There is risk.

In May 2017, Mandla Hlatshwayo and Oupa Duma, two prominent Black men in the South African entertainment industry, interrupted the scene of women being robbed outside a pub in Pimville. They did not know the women or their assailants as they left a trendy pub in Pimville, Soweto. Mandla Hlatshwayo, a former actor in the prime time soap opera *Generations*, who was a JoziFM DJ at the time of the incident, and his friend Oupa Duma were fatally shot for this interruption of the Female Fear Factory. Patriarchy is murderous. Interrupting it comes with a cost. However, patriarchy is always murderous even when we comply. The lie of safety is something I pay attention to in a later chapter, 'The False Promise of Safety.'

In this book, although I trace and illuminate diverse dimensions of the manufacture of female fear, I offer examples of its disruption in a variety of ways. I return in the chapter 'Fearing Feminists' to some other ways in which interrupting the manufacture of female fear is necessary, dangerous work.

Finally, although I initially developed the concept in relation to rape specifically, in the examples already provided, as well as in what follows, I show how the Female Fear Factory is a regulatory framework whose tools and promise of violence is not only rape. Although I had initially thought of the chapters of this book as distinct illustrations of specific aspects of the Female Fear Factory, I have been delighted by the numerous connections that have developed across chapters as I wrote.

Therefore, even as I outline the focus of the individual chapters below, drawing attention to some of these connections, it is my hope that even more overlaps will emerge as different readers interact with the book.

In chapter 1, I unpack the core ideas for this book: how certain categories of people are made female, what it means to think about fear as a political idea and a patriarchal product, and why 'factory' is the specific metaphor I use to think about the specific conditions and textures of its production.

Chapter 2 spends more time on fear, particularly how fear is taught, like a language in which patriarchy requires fluency. The Female Fear Factory cannot exist outside of fluency. However, because the word 'fluency' evokes so many disparate associations in different parts of the world, within scholarship, and depending on the linguistic landscapes of the place, I spend some time on the process of fluency and why fluency in fear matters.

Chapter 3 is dedicated to the dangerous fictions of the monstrous rapists and powerful men as benign, through an examination of the British television series, *Liar* and Salma Hayek's narrative of Harvey Weinstein's sexual terrorisation of her. In both these chapters, I write against these dangerous fictions.

Chapter 4 analyses 'mythologising misogyny' in the context of the Indian rape of Jyoti Singh and her naming as Nirbhaya, the fearless one, after a goddess. I ask: What does it mean to name her a fearless deity, when she was neither? I return to inversion of fear in chapter 9, 'Fearing Feminists,' to interrogate what sometimes happens to women who are publicly constructed as dangerous feminists when the patriarchal stakes are particularly high.

Chapter 5 reads against 'the false promise of safety,' perpetually deferred in various creative and seemingly 'commonsensical logics.' These are further expanded on in the chapters that follow, 'Femicidal Intimacy' (chapter 6) and 'Bodies of Knowledge' (chapter 7).

Chapter 8, 'Foreign Familiars,' turns to the site of South Africa's xenophobic violence for traces of the Female Fear Factory. Analysing short films by two of South Africa's most celebrated documentary filmmakers, Andy Spitz and Peabody awardee and twice-BAFTA winner, Xoliswa Sithole, I examine how the displaced women and girls they focus their cameras on speak against the Female Fear Factory in ways that suggest it functions similarly in different contexts.

The COVID-19 pandemic has refocused our attentions on fear in ways that bring power into even sharper focus. While there continue to be wide declarations of 'The New Normal,' there is much evidence of older structural configurations, sometimes repurposed for a new time. In chapter 10, I revisit the meanings of 'safety' and argue that COVID-19 times have ushered in a return to nationalism.

In place of a conclusion, I end on a personal diary, 'Refusing the Prison of Fear,' in which I map out my most enduring fears at different points in my life. It was not by design that so many journalists appear throughout this book as defiant, courageous, dissectors of patriarchal mythology. Yet, I found myself heavily reliant on a British feminist journalist's book and on documentaries by a Nigerian journalist, and a Salvadorian journalist in chapters on the dangerous fiction of the monstrous rapist, femicidal intimacy, and mythologising misogyny.

It is less surprising that I have relied on painting, documentary films, a television series, creative non-fiction, and a novel to think through some of my concerns and refine my concepts. The generative world of the imagination is my first love, and my best home. But as artist Penny Siopis reminds us in much of her work, home is very complicated terrain. From it springs joy, trauma, shame, connection and possibilities.

Stranger danger is such an entrenched part of our lives across cultures by now that the relationships between stranger and familiar recur in different chapters here too. From the neighbour who turns violent, to the femicidal partner, to the serial killer who would fit perfectly in a detective squad.

In each chapter, there are figures who fight powerfully against the Female Fear Factory. This is the first and most important task of the book you hold in your hand. To understand the Fear Factory so we can destroy it faster, more strategically and effectively, and, as much as possible, with feminist joy.

Interestingly, while I was writing this book, and taking regular walks to get some exercise and clear my mind, I had an encounter with the Female Fear Factory I had not spent too much time thinking about prior to this point. To be clear, I have always known that men attack women in public places, but to be charged at aggressively by a stranger with a weapon in the middle of the day was a surprise. I wish I could say that as he tried to hit me, I had pounced on him in self-defence, raining my fists on him like Mona Eltahawy and all the women who tweeted her their stories of beating their own attackers.

Alas, I simply stood my ground, and challenged him as he lunged at me. He never actually hit me, just threatened to with his body, several times. And although shocked and unnerved – not to mention weaponless – I neither cowered nor turned to run, although I did eventually get away from him.

This was less than a kilometre from my home, just before noon, in the suburb where I live very comfortably and where there are walkers, joggers, and dog walkers most times of the day. I suspect that my potential assailant had mental health challenges, because I offended him by waving as he smiled his greeting. I was wearing a mask. He accused me of hurling demons at him, and claimed to be poised to attack me and my demons.

When a young man who witnessed this public spectacle of the man repeatedly lunging at me stopped his car to offer me a getaway, my would-be assailant changed languages to very calmly address the young man. As a friend later remarked, patriarchy's enduring logic and men's investment in patriarchal privilege retains its grip even when all other logics are slippery. He had waved back at the man walking ahead of me a few minutes before I did the same. But he had lunged at me, sworn at me in our shared home language, hurling very gendered insults my way. When another man arrived at the scene, and a man whose linguistic ability he was uncertain of, he had calmly addressed him in English.

I was not terrorised. I still walk the same route.

# CHAPTER 1

# Manufacturing Female Fear

'Stories are nomadic.' – Jyoti Mistry and Antje Schuhmann[7]

The Female Fear Factory is ubiquitous across the globe. It is linked to rape, but not exclusively. To understand it requires grappling with its production sites and cycles, its languages, its stories, and its games. To this end, I bring together examples from different geographical spaces to show patterns, convergences, and how this sophisticated tool of control, the Female Fear Factory, is at once everywhere and yet can appear invisible. The stories through which I explore the Female Fear Factory are not examples for illustration. It is my hope that the stories themselves, as well as how I analyse them, using them to highlight facets of the patriarchal logic which undergirds fear, will enable recognition and widen strategies for anti-patriarchal work. In other words, because it is possible to see ourselves in the stories of others who are superficially nothing like ourselves, we can learn and imagine freeing ways of being. This is not true of just this book. Indeed, this is how stories always work.

When feminist film scholars Jyoti Mistry and Antje Schuhmann write of nomadic stories in the opening quotation to this chapter, this is some of what they are gesturing to. They are referring to the ability of the story to make sense at multiple levels as we encounter it: to appeal to our aesthetic sense, to enable us to make sense of something outside of the story itself, and to appeal to our capacity to imagine ourselves as connected to others – through empathy, recognition, and illumination. Therefore, the point is not to dwell on the fact of occupying identities other than those of the South African, Nigerian, US American, Saudi Arabian, Ugandan, Kenyan, Egyptian, British, El Salvadorian, Indian stories which are told here, but to recognise how critical it is to see both the sameness and peculiarities in how the Female Fear Factory manifests in different parts of the globe.

When I first came to theorise the manufacture of female fear, I was involved in a project of tracing the particular expressions of rape culture in South Africa. Such understanding was possible through painstaking scholarly attention to different South African historical epochs, lessons gleaned from three decades of feminist activism, conversation and reading, as well as more than four decades of living and seeing the world through feminist eyes. I am a lifelong student of feminist thinking and sensibility throughout the world. Therefore, I understood that I was writing a book on a particular aspect of patriarchal violence (rape) and illuminating specificities from a certain country (South Africa). At the same time, the phenomena I was studying were neither limited to rape nor my country. Rape is not possible without patriarchy. It is *for* patriarchy. Therefore, anti-rape work has to contribute to undoing patriarchy, or it is pointless. But patriarchy has a full violence toolkit where fear and shame have pride of place.

Fear is both an individual and a socio-political phenomenon.

At an individual level, fear can present as part of a healthy, well-developed warning system. Our ancestors across different societies learnt to fear certain things to ensure their own survival as individuals and as a species. This category of 'the feared' ranged from those in the physical realm (fire burns skin, lions may eat you, a stone or arrow can pierce skin and cause damage) to the more abstract (rejection hurts, there are consequences for our life decisions in the afterlife, crime). When we think about fear, it is important to hold in mind both notions of individual emotional experience and the political ways in which fear has been used in different epochs for control.

In both its individual and socio-political forms, fear is mnemonic. It is the memory of the lash on the plantation or on the factory floor (in the Industrial Revolution) that ultimately leads to compliance or revolt. It is also the memory of the lessons in fear that determine how women and queer people of different identifications may act in certain spaces. Paying attention to fear, its sites of generation, its targets, its beneficiaries, and the stories through which it is made sense of, helps us understand much about the structure of a society. Therefore, stories matter in and of themselves, but they also matter because they tell us something about the societies of their placement.

Patriarchy does not respect national boundaries. It is unabashedly promiscuous in its influences and tethers. Yet, it does use nationalism very productively. Therefore, as we watch patriarchy's use of fear, what is highlighted are both similarities across diverse societies and the textures that are specific to geopolitical entities. Women are produced very similarly, as is fluency in the Female Fear Factory, which I show elsewhere in this book. Yet even groups of feminists can carry the misguided identities that patriarchy exists less in their own countries than elsewhere. Patriarchy never travels alone. Its bedmates are capitalism, white supremacy, religious fundamentalism, and, increasingly, Islamophobia.

The late twentieth and early twenty-first centuries are rife with examples of conflict between feminists located in different parts of the world, and very often across the divides of North America and Western Europe, on one side, versus feminists located in parts of Africa, Asia, and Latin America on the other.

The root of this conflict is the age-old arrogance of empire, where those located at the heart of empire – even if they are not the most powerful within that empire – act out towards those outside the empire with the arrogance of power. The desire by northern and western European women to 'rescue' African women from female genital mutilation (FGM) is one such manifestation. The arrogance is fuelled by the way widespread, generations-deep feminisms by African women against FGM have been made invisible, as well as by the white saviour complex. Another example pertains to the ways in which US American women took up the mantle of #BringBackOurGirls, not in solidarity with the Nigerian feminist activists and lawyers who had long been in battle against the patriarchal religious fundamentalisms of Boko Haram in Nigeria with increasing success over many years, but in ways that actually endangered these efforts.

It did not occur to many of these feminists to pause and think about what solidarity might mean, what strategies were useful, and how their arrogant investment in 'visibility' rested on the erasure of local feminist work. The examples of this kind of feminist work that works against solidarity could fill a book.

That is not the task of this work.

However, the argument for internationalist feminisms and solidarity networks demands honest reflection, not romanticisation of feminist intent. Even for feminist women, sisterhood may be possible, but it is not automatic. It is chosen and earned in processes that are as reflective as they are committed.

This is not a paradox.

## Making the Female

In introductory undergraduate classes on gender and sexuality, significant time is spent on distinguishing between the concepts of 'sex' and 'gender.' This is important work for a variety of reasons. Much of this energy is spent on distinguishing between sex as biological marker and gender as a social one, since feminists have long established that language is never just an innocent carrier of ideas. It is also how those ideas are made and how they travel. I now turn to the important body of work by feminists differently located that has assisted us to understand the difference between gender and sex, before attending to the dangerous work that happens when we collate the two. There is enormous value in interrogating what we take for granted when we teach this distinction, and in interrogating what we assume is an 'error' in the slippage between the two categories in everyday contexts. Spending some time first on what that work of distinguishing between biological sex and social gender has taught us is important, so we understand what is under discussion. The feminists on which I draw have historically come to very similar illuminations even though they come at the problem from very different disciplines and sites of study.

Further to this, I want to make another argument, building on these. When we make this distinction, we often assume that people who say 'female' when they mean 'woman' are making a mistake because they do not understand (or accept) the difference between the biological and the social. In many instances, this is the case, because patriarchy relies on the conflation of the two. However, while accepting the difference as crucial, we also need to recognise that this slippage is not always *only* accidental misreading, but rather another way in which the patriarchal conflation is repeatedly enacted. In other words, it is both a lie, and the social linguistic way in which it is being normalised, rendered as true. This is because language does not (just) describe the world; it makes the world. Therefore, one of the ways in which something *becomes* true is through repetition. Consequently, it is important both to recognise the error and to be attentive to what the repetition of the error – wilfully or otherwise – creates.

In the introductory chapter to his book *Culture and Imperialism*, Edward Said reminds us that '[t]he power to narrate, or to block other narratives from forming and emerging, is very important to culture and imperialism, and constitutes one of the main connections between them.'[8] Any deep attention to how empire works shows that language has materiality, that stories are not 'just words.' The power to name, define, and delineate is not abstract.

Historically, it has shaped the world through law, the academy, war, stop and search, checkpoints, reservations, auctions, genocide, rape, and nationalism. To simply state, for example, that 'race is a social construct' does not actually mean that it is not real. For a species that *is* social, the contents of our chromosomes cannot be the dominant definition of the 'real.' It meant precious little to us as Black people under apartheid to know that race was not biologically real. It gives the families of Native American women (who disappear and are never properly investigated or found) and Palestinians no comfort and is totally useless for the African

American who is stopped for driving while Black. It is not just frustrating but also violent to be reminded of this state of being a social construction, as though this is not real. Humans are social beings. Therefore, a social construct is more real than what really lies in our genetic make-up when we are trying to understand society, power, and the ways in which people behave.

The existence of race as real may have started out as a lie. However, over the last five hundred years, it has been created in the same way that human beings create anything: through the imagination and repetition, through language, through performance, through proceeding as though it were true, through enforcement and violence. It has to be possible to recognise both the colonial, white supremacist historic lie – since race is still not in our genes – and the ways in which the world has been remade in consistently violent ways (and resisted in proliferating activisms) so that race matters.

Race is not analogous to sex and gender. They intersect and are co-constitutive in their various mutations. The world of white supremacy, the world through which race was made to matter, used sexual violence as a tool.

The gains of global feminist organising and thinking have persistently reminded us that the binary sex/gender logic of patriarchy is not descriptive, but inscriptive, an attempt to create a world that has two distinct and oppositional genders which are determined by information located in our chromosomes (biology).

Feminist scholarship that critiques the patriarchal conflation of sex and gender, the logic of 'biology as destiny,' also called 'anatomy as destiny,' abounds. Full-length studies that contribute to this vast body of work from different locations in the 1980s include Genevieve Lloyd's 1984 *The Man of Reason: 'Male' and 'Female' in Western Philosophy*; Gloria Anzaldua's 1987 *Borderlands/La Frontera*; Ifi Amadiume's 1987 *Male Daughters, Female Husbands*; Joan Smith's *Misogynies* in 1989; and Diana Scully and Pauline Bart's 1978 shorter critique of the development of gynaecology's (and psychiatry's) historic misogyny from the nineteenth century, in their influential essay 'A Funny Thing Happened on the Way to the Orifice.'

These feminist texts are not representative but rather offer a sample of positions from which patriarchy's lie has been exposed. This unmasking can be traced in even older documents that use autobiographical and analytical strategies we would readily recognise as feminist today, in early twentieth-century texts as well as older writing such as Sojourner Truth's 'Ain't I a Woman?' speech; abolitionist Mary Prince's *History of Mary Prince, a West Indian Slave*, first published in 1831; or Crimean war nurse Mary Seacole's *The Wonderful Adventures of Mrs Seacole in Many Lands*, published in 1857 – all of whom rejected white supremacist, patriarchal biological definitions and subsequent mythologised limitations on them as Blackwomen.

In wide-ranging ways, these books – and thousands of feminist articles in the twentieth century – have established the centrality of the logic of 'biology-as-destiny' theory for patriarchal violence and control. In *The Creation of Patriarchy*, Lerner writes:

> Many feminists argue that the limited number of proven biological differences *among* the sexes have been vastly exaggerated by cultural interpretations and the value put on sex differences is in itself a cultural product. Sexual attributes are a biological given, but gender is a product of historical process.[9] (Emphasis mine.)

In other words, a difference, once inflated, is cast as a relation of antagonism, exaggerating the differences that exist *among* sexes as those that exist *between* the sexes: a binary. The overstatement of these differences between male and female is not due to their actual existence so much as it is for cultural and historic importance. Exaggerating these sex differences now cast as binary opposites, as well as attaching meaning to them through gender roles and valuation systems, is a historic process. Patriarchy has created this sex difference between sexes using the logic of the biological in order to be able to create meaning that amplifies what can be supported in biological sex. To do this, sex has been crystallised in cultural processes to create rigid and exaggerated binary gender difference. Binary thinking is about valuation; Lerner importantly uses 'among the sexes' rather than the patriarchal 'between the sexes.' The exaggeration of biological difference is the first step in creating the myth of two sexes, which is then easily translated into the two genders with self-evident (binary) differences, patriarchally speaking. Patriarchal biologist logic renders these binaries in sex and gender as automatic. However, we would be wise to recall that the move from difference to duality to binary thinking is not an automatic transition, but a constructed one. Crucially, binary opposition is more than duality: it is also opposition, competition, and hierarchical valuation.

This is an important point to remake, especially at a time when the global backlash against feminist gains again attempts not only to trap us in the old logic of 'two sexes' that equal 'two genders' as norm, but also to reduce agency to free-floating choice. Even though the word 'backlash' has been so corrupted that it can sometimes mean any antagonistic response, it is important to remember that Susan Faludi coined it to refer to the relentless, institutionalised, violent undoing of feminist work and gains.

In *Backlash: The Undeclared War against American Women*, Faludi offers important reminders that erasure of feminist gains, thought, and activism is part of its trivialisation. Backlash is not mere pushback; it is erasure and, as Faludi's subtitle shows, is a war against feminism and women. If we have no awareness of feminist arguments, strategies, and ways of thinking in generations prior to our own, it is also easier to dismiss wholesale the complex threads that got us here, including traditions of engagement across differences that deliberately eschewed binary thinking.

Pioneering Black feminist novelist, short story writer and essayist Miriam Tlali reminds us that history offers lessons that some struggles are not new, and that we would be wise to consider how previous generations of revolutionaries have confronted recurring problems. More recently, Jane Bennett, in her essay 'Credibility, Plausibility and Autobiographical Oral Narrative,' has argued that the disappearance of awareness of feminist traditions of thought from yesteryear is deliberately orchestrated patriarchal gymnastics that trivialise and ultimately make invisible the ways in which feminists of previous generations have painstakingly sought to unmask the biologist logic of the male, even if that logic is still in operation.

In other words, according to Bennett, it is no accident that many younger feminists are ignorant of how fiercely contested and rigorously crafted many feminist gains, concepts, and strategies were in previous eras. While generations of feminists have always known the importance of creating alternate knowledge, we may have underestimated the enduring power of patriarchal erasure.

This places Bennett's thinking as a very important expansion and re-theorisation of the backlash against feminist thought. In various spoken engagements, including as a panellist at the 2018 International Women's Day lecture hosted by the University of South Africa (UNISA) and the Thabo Mbeki Foundation, veteran ANC leader Thenjiwe Mtintso has argued that it is the backlash, rather than confusion or contradictions, that explains rising misogyny in different parts of the globe. One of the areas in which the logic of the male retains its grip is in the worldwide Female Fear Factory, the subject of this book.

In a linked vein, Tommaso Milani begins his essay 'Querying the Queer from Africa' with this reflection on how binaries work to enshrine:

> The gender binary – the distinction between males and females as complementary and desirable opposites – is constantly produced through everyday, apparently "banal" practices. Such process is not innocuous but is part and parcel of hegemonic ideological formations of gender and sexuality that contribute to positioning some individuals as "normal"

and "desirable" whilst recasting others as "unwanted" and "deviant."[10]

Milani's use of language is instructive here. The deliberate use of 'distinction' and 'constantly produced' are warnings against the success of patriarchal elision of this constant construction – rather than description – of difference. Relentless and innocuous creation of sex difference as binary serves to naturalise the violence of patriarchy in creating the categories of male and female.

Failure to recognise the 'hegemonic ideological formations' is patriarchal success. Therefore, the Female Fear Factory is not a synonym for the 'women fear factory' because 'female' does not 'woman' equal. Female, here, is the site of the 'hegemonic ideological formations' Milani writes against. The Female Fear Factory relies on patriarchal, biologist logic and needs to be named as such.

The manufacture of female fear is not a feminist phenomenon, even if its unmasking is; it is a patriarchal phenomenon that must be constantly confronted. Its critique here and elsewhere in my work is the feminist project. No feminist project has any hope without clarifying its analytical tools. The targets of the Female Fear Factory are *all* women, not as a natural target, but because they have been made female. The Female Fear Factory is also for those who are not women, but who have been ideologically constructed as female.

I make no apologies for focusing on how patriarchy terrorises women, because we are always rendered as female, even as I repeatedly return to how patriarchy provisionally creates others in female register through violence.

Humans – all women, some men, and sexual minorities – are made socially female through a series of experiential processes. It is important to think about the body and embodiment as socially constituted, rather than as pre-existing and/or immutable.

Indeed, as Bibi Bakare-Yusuf reminds us in her essay 'Beyond Determinism: The Phenomenology of African Female Existence,' 'agency and experience are not fixed or given in advance.' They are not ready-made, stable categories. Rather, they are situational, and as such, 'continuously being re-constituted and open to changing contexts' which account for embodied agency. Put differently, our actions and experiences are shaped by context, and take on different meanings depending on conditions, time, and place. She continues:

> This account of embodied agency means that my identity as an African woman is not pre-determined by biology, social norms or regulative practices. Who I am and who I become are shaped by my actions and choices to resist, rework or acquiesce to bio-cultural normativity (Allen, 1989). From this perspective, the body is understood as a situation, with this implying both freedom and constraint in the ongoing dialogue between world and embodied agent. The meaning of "African woman" becomes material, embodied, multiple and generative, rather than a disembodied abstraction.[11]

In other words, the body matters in multiple, potentially infinite ways, not in closed-off or preordained ones. To speak of the body as 'a situation' is an elegant way of simultaneously drawing attention to how eventful (arrives and is generative) and located it is, in a specific place. Reading Bakare-Yusuf's thinking of embodiment as situational, processual, and generative, then, also illuminates how the Female Fear Factory presents itself differently on the body as experienced by those read as female, and the multiple possibilities for imagining freedom against 'bio-cultural normativity,' the tyranny of patriarchal 'anatomy as destiny.'

Furthermore, in this book I probe, along with Bakare-Yusuf, not just the ways in which fear is entangled in the situational body marked as female, but also:

> How does bodily being affect and shape the kind of experience we can have? Why are the bodily beings of women and men used to demarcate social difference? What limitations and

> liberties does a woman face on account of her encounter with the world as a female?[12]

Put differently, I probe how specific bodies are interpreted in ways that shape experiences both oppressive and enabling. I investigate how bodies are made to matter in patriarchal ways – as tablets on which to inscribe control through fear, as disposable – or through generative and/or disruptive feminist strategies. And in juxtaposing patriarchal violence and feminist strategy, both subjected to consistent feminist analysis and abstraction, I develop a language to speak against a global phenomenon without universalising logic.

## Dramatising the Female

As I write this, the process through which those who challenge patriarchal biologist definitions can be rendered as 'female' is being dramatised in a popular South African soap opera, *The Queen*. For several weeks, a central character, Luntu, nicknamed 'Schumacher' by his friends, is an openly bisexual character who has been in several relationships and has experienced casual sexual encounters in previous episodes. He is played by the actor Vuyolwethu Ngcukana. Recently, Buntu (played by Phila Madlingozi), Schumacher's younger brother, has made an appearance, as several aspects of their shared backstory are revealed. Schumacher has made a life for himself in Johannesburg, and his younger brother's arrival destabilises this new life by revealing the physically abusive father and traumatic childhood from which they have both fled.

Although they initially bond over their respective escapes, their new relationship falls apart when Buntu realises what his father meant when he insisted the beating would turn him into 'a real man,' and ensure he was nothing like his older brother. Schumacher confides in his friends, Thato and Mzekezeke, that his father could see 'who' and 'how' he really was. This is an important recognition. Luntu/Schumacher is not what is often called 'effeminate,' so this is not what the father has seen.

However, his erotic and romantic interest in men, his preference for long reflection rather than violence to resolve matters, and his innate curiosity, rather than hostility, towards encounters with difference aggravates their father. The younger brother has not yet arrived at the total rejection of violence. Although critical of outright brutality, and traumatised by it, he still holds that violence and aggression have an important role to play in how men relate to and interact with other men. He is similarly accepting of the scripts of obligatory heterosexuality and hetero-patriarchy. As the conflict escalates between the two brothers, the language used is telling.

For Luntu/Schumacher, the father's brutality is finally understandable, due to Schumacher's failure at hegemonic masculinity. Using the predictable slurs against gay men, Buntu insists that Schumacher is *like* a woman, female. In the brothers' exchanges, Schumacher repeatedly refers to his completion and seamless mastery of ulwaluko, the Xhosa masculinity initiation rituals, euphemistically called isiko (the tradition). The older brother insists that it is homophobia itself that is at odds with the traditional values passed on to initiates. As there is no available way to legitimately unmake a man, the older brother's refusal to be rendered 'like a woman' or symbolically female can only be met with anger by Buntu.

Importantly, the inferred source of repulsion from the father is the failure of sons to be properly men, or men in the full sense. The younger son's embattlement contains echoes of the father's distaste tempered with a deep affection for Schumacher. The fact of the older brother's aversion to violence and his bisexuality brings the younger brother to near crisis. His 'woman-like' brother is not what Buntu expected. Importantly, according to his father, and initially his brother, Schumacher 'ubufazarha': he is 'woman-like.' He is not characterised 'umfazi' or even 'ibhinqa,' a woman. He is not even 'womanish.' To be 'woman-like' is to belong to a category that can be treated like women, what I call being made female here. To be womanish is to exhibit behaviour conventionally associated with women.

'Womanish' has positive associations in feminist language after Alice Walker's delineation of how she comes to 'womanist' in *In Search of Our Mothers' Gardens: Womanist Prose*:

> From *womanish.* (Opp. of 'girlish', i.e., frivolous, irresponsible, not serious). A black feminist or feminist of color. From the black folk expression of mothers to female children, 'you acting womanish', i.e., like a woman. Usually referring to outrageous, audacious, courageous or *willful* behavior. Wanting to know more and in greater depth than is considered 'good' for one. Interested in grown up things. Acting grown up. Being grown up. Interchangeable with another black folk expression: 'You trying to be grown.' Responsible. In charge. *Serious.*[13]

Schumacher is not womanish. He has also successfully undergone the series of rituals to make him a man in Xhosa cosmology. Therefore, the difficulty Schumacher poses for his brutal father, and his brutalised homophobic brother, is a crisis of legitimacy.

He refuses their attempts to shame him, or un-man him, by insisting that a bisexual man is still a man. And because seniority is authority, it is the younger homophobic brother who is in crisis, because no matter how deep-seated his homophobia is, he cannot ally himself with the monster father. He also recognises isiko, the process through which people are made men in the Xhosa world, as legitimate. To recognise ulwaluko, or isiko, as sacred means accepting that Schumacher is in fact a man, and one with seniority over him.

Violence always creates something in the world. Both brothers are traumatised by a father's physical brutality and his attempts to make them into something specific: the father's vision of legitimately aggressive masculinity. This patriarchal violence is explicitly a way to make the sons 'proper men,' and symbolically male. It produces different results: Luntu escapes to a fulfilling, honest life of his own making as Schumacher, whereas Buntu initially re-enacts masculine violence through his misogyny and homophobia. Buntu remains haunted by his father's justification for the beatings – an attempt to erase any sign that they may be anything but 'male' and full, proper men.

Furthermore, in this particular narrative arc, it is Schumacher's life and identity that is sympathetically portrayed. Unlike Buntu, who battles for legitimacy, Schumacher has mastered additional sites of complex and affirming masculinity. He has deep friendships with two emotionally sophisticated heterosexual men, and is gainfully employed in a trucking company doing physically demanding work, signalled by the two-piece royal blue coverall uniform he dons during working hours.

The struggle between father and sons is a struggle over masculine legitimacy. Schumacher understands what it means to be rendered not 'woman,' but 'woman-like,' which is to say 'female,' as do his friends, who are enraged by the suggestion and defend his masculinity against accusations of being 'woman-like,' female.

These same friends also consistently stand as women's allies in other parts of the narrative arc. Thus, while Schumacher's friends defend him against accusations that he is not a man, they do not ordinarily care to police the boundaries of manhood. Indeed, the three friends, Schumacher, Thato, and Mzekezeke, have shared values and occupy different versions of masculinity that coexist without conflict in most of the soap opera's arcs.

Much more could be written about the exchanges and contests for masculinity, against being constructed as 'woman-like' in this unfolding narrative; what is clear in what continues to unfold is the manner in which people can be rendered female through violence, terror, and fear.

In order to understand this crucial distinction, we have to reject the patriarchal seduction that naturalises female/sex into women/gender. We have to understand how the Female Fear Factory works to keep women and 'females' terrified, as well as how it uses the patriarchal fear of women and all females to justify violence against women. The boys' father legitimises his abuse through marking them as females, and his desire to make them into proper men. He continues to subject his sons to the kind of disciplining violence that is permitted for women and others made 'female,' but not for proper, full Xhosa men.

Like Jyoti Mistry and Antje Schumann, as a feminist academic located within the South African academy, in my 'understanding of gender as a social construct [I] problematise hegemonic gaze regimes seeing sex, seeing bodies, as organised along the "natural" binary of being *either* male *or* female.'[14]

## An Anatomy of Fear

Fear is both an individual emotional experience and a very particular public phenomenon. In *Fear: The History of a Political Idea*, Corey Robin traces the historic development of fear as a very peculiar political construction. Robin shows how the political and social uses of fear are very closely tied to what appear to be merely personal experiences of fear, writing that where aspects of fear appear personal whilst actually being political, '[t]hey spring from pervasive social inequities, and help sustain long traditions of rule over women and workers.'[15]

Fear is part of the patriarchal and capitalist machinery that sets up and maintains traditions of oppression and containment. Fear thus deployed emerges from reinforced traditions and legitimised authority through legal rules over centuries. In this sense, then, it is possible to speak about fear as both experiential and institutional. Since fear 'arises from the social, political and economic hierarchies that divide people, its special function is internal "intimidation" where a group's communicated threats protect another group's power at the expense of the former,'[16] as Robin reminds us. Seen like this, then, fear is an integral part of maintaining power. In the case of the Saudi Arabian women's 'right to drive' activists, this deliberate use of fear to maintain men's power in that country is evident.

Although they come at the phenomenon of collective fear from a very different direction, Maria Jarymowicz and Daniel Bar-Tal's theorisation of the intersections of personal and collective public fear rhyme with Robin's.

In their essay, 'The Dominance of Fear over Hope in the Life of Individuals and Collectives,' Jarymowicz and Bar-Tal define fear as 'an automatic emotion based on past and present affective experiences,'[17] clarifying that it 'is processed both unconsciously and consciously.' In addition to its personal and political dimensions (which they insist should be read simultaneously rather than as competitive, much like Robin proposes), they point to the very important way in which fear leads to specific ways of processing information. Jarymowicz and Bar-Tal write, 'Emotions serve as mediators and as data for processing of feelings, judgement, evaluation, and decision making that may then lead to particular behaviours.'[18]

Jarymowicz and Bar-Tal importantly draw our attention to the manner in which prolonged exposure leads to a 'collective emotional orientation' due to:

> particular common experiences, socialization, and conditions in society, which include exposure to common information, discourses, symbols, models, epistemic authorities, emphases, values, norms, narratives, beliefs, attitudes, influences, and learning.[19]

In other words, 'prolonged exposure' to direct teaching about the dangers that await if women behave in certain ways; witnessing the treatment of others when they live in interesting ways or are seen to 'step out of line'; the repetition of ideas about proper gender in symbolic sites, school, family, religious sites lead to the 'collective emotional orientation' to fear. These sites inculcate fluency and reinforce the Female Fear Factory by producing and reproducing it until fear becomes the collective experience of women in many societies.

## Factories and Fear

Factories are a specific mode of production, emerging in the Industrial Revolution, out of money garnered through the slave trade. The specific conditions of their emergence are important for the metaphoric way in which I put 'factory' to work in this book. The emergence of factories – and with them capitalism – is characterised by specific dimensions and articulations of power important for my work here. These include coercion, accumulation, injustice, and massification. At the same time, as I choose 'factory,' it is important to remember that there have been other forms of production and exchange that predate capitalism but which are not useful here.

I use 'factory' here metaphorically. Like all metaphors, it works up to a certain point; it has limited utility. It is important to bear in mind that while patriarchy may have found wonderful bedfellows in capitalism and white supremacy, whose creation it is implicated in, it predates them. Therefore, as we never lose sight of intersectional analysis, we should guard against the trap of imagining that undoing capitalism will automatically do anti-patriarchal work, since we have ample evidence of patriarchal, pre-capitalist societies.

Secondly, much postcolonial scholarship over the second half of the twentieth century has illustrated how crucial sexual violence was to the creation of empire, universalising the association between rape and warfare, where it had previously been limited to Europe, violently making it logical and appear as though it has always been the way wars were fought by Africans, Asians, and Americans in centuries before.

With all that said, successful deployment of the metaphor of the factory requires time spent on the historical rise of the factory as the dominant mode of production. I find Leslie Salzinger's reminder that factories produce not just products but also workers 'like all effective arenas of production' important here. Consequently, then, in *Genders in Production*, she underscores the importance of making visible the 'connections between the production of subjects and the production of commodities.'[20] This rendering visible is crucial to shining light on factories and their machinations, unmasking the mythologisation and romance in which they have been couched as capitalism gained ground.

How, then, is the worker produced? The workforce did not naturally – or easily – take to the new forms and conditions of work in the Industrial Revolution. In the essay 'Factory Discipline in the Industrial Revolution,' Sidney Pollard writes that factories had to use force to construct 'the regularity and discipline'[21] of work. Discipline was enforced through the creation of various forms of supervision. For Salzinger, 'labour control was already expressed and enforced through multiple hierarchies of watching and watched' through supervision that 'always involves shaping others,'[22] ensuring that '[d]ocility, no matter who exhibits it, is produced on the shop floor, not acquired ready-made.'[23] In other words, the worker may have been responsible for creating objects (products) for market, but she was herself a product in the making through constant supervision.

To expound on this notion of 'supervision' and its forming ability à la Salzinger, I turn again to Pollard, for further clarification. Reading Pollard, it becomes clear that the mild-sounding 'supervision' took on a variety of forms. In the change to meanings of 'labour' to 'accumulation' and 'obedience,' many factory owners relied on 'deliberate or accidental modellings of … workhouses and prisons, a fact well known to the working population'[24] that understood the connections between factory work and bondage.

By the late 1700s, a series of strategies – including 'time-thrift,' 'constant attendance,' and 'work rules' – to break the preferences of the labour force, were introduced and formalised.

In 1821, in the flax mills in Britain, everyone – managers, overseers, mechanics, oilers, spreaders, spinners, and reelers – had their particular duty pointed out to them. If they transgressed, they were instantly turned off as unfit for their situation.

It was so important to create obedience and docility that both carrot and stick methods were formally and explicitly discussed as such, well into the middle of the nineteenth century. Where the carrot included the still familiar inducements such as more pay, promotions, rewards and, less conventionally for our times, snuff, it was in the stick that the real brutality was exposed. The stick included corporal punishment, dismissals and fines, as well as shaming and humiliation. The connections between shaming and factories are long-standing ones.

Finally, when we remember that until well into the 1840s in Britain and in other places, the labourer being produced included children, the suitability of the metaphor is further driven home. To drive this point further, and to link forward to the discussion of shame, childhood and fear, Pollard relates a story of how, as part of shaming, in Bradford, children who were hard to render docile were made to write their offence on a large card, hold it up, and walk up and down the road or factory floor.

In the chapters that follow, different aspects of the production of both workers and products of the Female Fear Factory receive concentrated attention.

In *Rape: A South African Nightmare*, I wrote that the Female Fear Factory requires many bodies, minds, and numerous components to ensure that the conveyor belt moves through successive stations without interruption. These stations alter the product on the conveyor belt slightly, but are part of the same process of repetition and product modification. In a unidirectional operation, with a clear product as the ultimate outcome, there are dangers that accompany interference with the production process. Unceremonious interruptions not only cause havoc but may very well lead to maiming, loss of limbs – or even prove to be fatal.

In recent times, as the world grapples with the COVID-19 pandemic, the logic of the economy as superior to the health and safety considerations of human beings has found repeated circulation. It was found everywhere in arguments against lockdowns. In the first few months of the 2020 COVID-19 pandemic, in countries such as the US, Brazil, and the UK, presidents espoused approaches to the pandemic that sought to prioritise market pressures and demands, rather than minimise the risk of virus transmissions at the cost of the economy. These presidents resisted lockdowns and other measures as excessive, sometimes downplayed the toll the virus was taking, even in their own countries, and ignored the rising numbers of casualties in favour of alternative explanations for what is unfolding across the globe. There were some significant changes in attitude to lockdowns in the latter part of 2020 in parts of the US, as well as in the UK.

In their earlier stances, these presidents explicitly prioritised the vibrancy of the economy at the cost of human life, predicting the real crisis would be a collapsed economy, holding these predictions as self-evident truths regardless of appeals from science and health communities. In the case of the US, global readers and audiences have been astounded to see groups protesting all manner of coronavirus safety measures, seemingly oblivious to the high numbers of infection and mortality rates in their own country.

COVID-19 has highlighted an already existing logic: factories and industry are the backbone of the capitalist economy; the economy is the most important consideration; and human life is disposable. Under capitalist economies, the most disempowered workers are the hardest working ones; they are the easiest to replace, receive the lowest compensation for their labour and, in old Marxist terms, own neither the product nor the 'means of production,' that is, the process of its creation, distribution, and sale.

The Female Fear Factory reminds us that all women are safe to violate, are beatable, and are killable. This is what it means to be female in this context, which is to say, as having feminine value in a patriarchal hierarchical worldview. It means to be legitimately domitable and ultimately disposable, which is not contradicted by the centrality of women's labour (as work and as reproduction), in the regeneration of patriarchal societies.

To be female is to also be excessive and therefore legitimately kept under control, through both violence and the threat of violence. Indeed, under patriarchy, violence is simultaneously ever present and promised. To be domitable is also to be penetrable, where this assumes and demands passive piercing as preferable.

To be female is to be conquerable. It is no coincidence that acts and narratives of war speak of 'conquered land' in feminine terms and use feminine pronouns, and of subjugated, violated land as 'raped' land.

# CHAPTER 2

## Fear, Fluency and Control

'I was thinking all the time that shall I put a knife under my pillow? The time was of fear, but some people can overcome fear and some people can fight.' – Malala Yousafzai[25]

'Apparently fear is expected of women.' – Caroline Paul[26]

When author and former firefighter Caroline Paul finds herself constantly confronted with questions about whether her line of work frightens her, she is never confused about the difference between the way she is confronted with these questions versus the very different way her colleagues, who are men, are asked questions about their work. In this chapter, I endorse her statement that 'fear is expected of women,' recognising this as a sentiment that will be familiar to women across the world. Beyond agreement, however, I am interested in how this expectation – which is a test of fluency on the Female Fear Factory – is set up. To do so, it is important to pause and reflect on fluency, its meanings, its processes, and its expectations.

Language is simultaneously a most mundane and most complicated aspect of human life. As such, then, fluency is both home and minefield. When I initially wrote of rape as a language and fluency as an integral part of how fear is reproduced and normalised, I imagined myself to be saying something quite straightforward. I live in a part of the world where speaking multiple languages from different language family groups is the norm. It is an experience I share with people from many – albeit not all – other societies that live in the shadow of colonialism.

To speak multiple languages brings with it the awareness that language is not just a carrier of meaning and values, but also a means of access to very specific realms of possibility. This is not a matter of words and concepts. When I say the words 'family' and 'home' in English or German, I mean something radically different from what I evoke when I say the linguistic equivalent in isiXhosa. This difference is so much more than the easily available gradations of nuclear and extended, birth, marital, or chosen family. While translation is always possible, a polyglot understands that what is transferred may be planet-wide, but what is lost is oceans-deep.

Incompleteness is not impossibility. It is the playground of the imagination for those who occupy language multiverses. In South Africa, an inordinate amount of time is spent privately and in public discourse on the many ways in which language is political, contesting what things mean, discussing proper and inappropriate ways of occupying language, and accent (as emphasis, as a way to place a speaker socially, or both).

We understand that fluency is not a final destination, but a range of positions. Even as a child, I laughed when I watched US films about undercover agents who learn a language in a few months, travel to the USSR, and convince mother-tongue speakers that they are one of them. Even as an adult, each time I encounter this in a film, my suspended disbelief is interrupted, and I am made aware that this is a product of a mono- or bilingual imagination. Polyglots know that fluency does not a mother-tongue accent create. Because home is not a 'permanently unchangeable address'[27] (to use Pier Paolo Frassinelli's wonderful phrase), there are many ways to feel 'at home' in a language. To feel at home in a language is to attain fluency, but this fluency is a continuum. I will return to this briefly, below.

Importantly, it is not simply the biographical fact of being able to take up home in different homes that availed fluency as a framework for explaining aspects of the Female Fear Factory. My formal exposure to linguistics as a discipline has been minimal. Combined training in literary theory and fluency in five languages, basic conversational skills in a sixth, and an inability to learn a seventh despite bombarding it with willpower for two years, mean that I have complicated experiences of fluency.

It is precisely this migratory perspective on fluency that clarifies the way initially rape, and now, the Female Fear Factory, makes sense as a language. In patriarchal societies, we are socialised into the Female Fear Factory in ways similar to how we are made fluent in language.

Before I turn to what scholarship teaches us about fluency, I want to discuss how we are conditioned into different kinds of fluency. It can be a very slippery word. For many bilingual people, it seems to mean command and mastery of a language. For many polyglots, it can mean significantly more than this.

## Fluency, Homes, and Landmines

The four languages in which I had attained fluency by the time I left primary school are windows into distinct conceptual universes. They also messily reach across boundaries to intersect or collide in numerous ways. I speak three of them regularly and with abandon, but choose when to converse in the fourth carefully, for political reasons. By the time I was twenty, I had been formally taught two additional languages. I completely failed to master the sixth. In the end it lay discarded with no regrets.

In my late twenties, I would acquire a replacement sixth language in a foreign country I lived in for a few years. I am not at home in it, and do not watch films, read novels or attend theatre productions in it, like I do with the others, but I can make myself understood in conversation, read instructions, complete forms, and watch the news in it.

There are possible explanatory bridges for the rate of acquisition patterns. In high school, the new language (isiZulu) which I was taught linguistically and studied literature in, belonged to the same cluster as one of my mother tongues. When I started learning German, the grammatical structure and rules of Afrikaans I had learned made a significant difference.

The language and fluency landscape I want to evoke, then, is a continuum. On the one end, fluency encompasses feelings of ease, where language can be a place of ease (home). On the other end exists enough familiarity to function well in it, but it is emotionally fraught (a landmine).

Let me turn to what the scholars of language and fluency have to say about the terrain. Francine Chambers points out that even among linguists there are variances in the accepted understandings of fluency. In her essay, 'What Do We Mean by Fluency?' she distinguishes between 'lay' understandings of fluency as referring to 'overall oral proficiency' in a language on the one hand, and the more academic definitions among language researchers – most of whom are concerned with 'efficient processes of speech production'[28] – and advanced progress in language learning on the other. In other words, within linguistics, 'fluency' signals a very high competence in a language as seen from demonstrated ability to comprehend, articulate, and function in a language.

Taking this a step further, the title of John Pikulski and David Chard's article, 'Fluency: The Bridge from Decoding to Reading Comprehension,' reveals even more about the processes of fluency, as well as the connections between different processes. Pikulski and Chard write:

> Reading fluency refers to rapid, efficient, accurate word recognition skills that permit a reader to construct the meaning of a text. Fluency is also manifested in accurate, rapid, expressive oral reading and is applied during, and makes possible, silent reading comprehension.[29]

In other words, it is not only recognition and comprehension that matter. They explain that fluency is achieved when you can recognise the words quickly, accurately discern meaning ('identification-decoding') and successfully articulate yourself ('comprehension-meaning construction') in a specific language.

They further clarify that a 'non-fluent' person is one who has 'not yet developed automatic decoding skills,' and therefore hesitates, repeats the same process, or is unable to attain accuracy.

While many scholars who write on fluency focus on speech, Pikulski and Chard's stress on reading fluency is particularly important for understanding fluency as it works in the Female Fear Factory. This is especially the case if we substitute 'sign' for 'words' in the passage below:

> Constructing meaning involves making inferences, responding critically, and so on, and it always requires attention. The nonfluent reader can alternate attention between the two processes; however, this makes reading a laborious, often punishing process. If attention is drained by decoding words, little or no capacity is available for the attention-demanding process of comprehending. Therefore, automaticity of decoding—a critical component of fluency—is essential for high levels of reading achievement.[30]

Applying the above, fluency in the Female Fear Factory requires interpreting and clustering signs into 'meaningful thought units,' activating background knowledge and existing knowledge, and acting accordingly. Those people who are not fluent in the Female Fear Factory may focus on minutiae and miss the overall messages performed for their benefit. This can occur in cases where we are confronted with unfamiliar cultures, although the Female Fear Factory is a global phenomenon.

Although there is wide variance of opinion on how fluency is achieved, many other scholars, such as Roxanne Hudson, offer a combination of the approaches above, and numerous theories, to explain the processes and make suggestions on how best to teach in order to ensure learners achieve fluency. There is nonetheless relative consensus among scholars that fluency is achieved once the process of discerning and making meaning is 'effortless,' 'fast,' 'remembered,' and confirmed by other aspects of context.

These scholars also agree that fluency is achieved through explicit teaching, repetition, modelling, coaching, and prolonged exposure. Linking back to the Female Fear Factory more explicitly, patriarchal societies teach a specific logic around gender. For example, ideas about boys and girls are very different, and specific realms of what is permissible are often taught to children as lessons and as correction. Adults in various contexts will often teach these lessons to children, which range from the seemingly mild ('sit like a girl') to the aggressive ('dress like you want to be treated'). As children watch people around them perform gender in specific ways, including what to tolerate ('boys will be boys'), they also learn how to behave in accordance with patriarchal norms.

To think about fluency in the Female Fear Factory in line with the scholarship above brings to light several dimensions. Fluency in fear requires exposure through repetition of messages, warning, inducements, symbolic lessons, and explicit statements. Such exposure eventually inures a person to the environment, which eventually becomes easier and easier to decipher. Consequently, she is able to read, decode messages quickly and effortlessly, not for individual attention but as a smooth process of communication.

To refer back to examples already used in this book, when Saudi women repeatedly witness and are exposed to the consequences of their driving, and are warned against the dangers of women driving, many understand that they are not meant to drive, in a process that carries threats of imprisonment, deepening confinement, and social exclusion. Similarly, the university student who spoke up in my class has learnt that danger lies everywhere, and this influences how she navigates the streets, by not responding to every encounter she has with sexual harassment. It is not only compliance that sees women ignore street harassment some of the time, it is also fluency in what those threats mean and how quickly that violence can escalate in public view. As Jennifer Wright writes in 'Women Are Afraid Men Will Murder Them,' 'by the time women reach sexual maturity, pretty much every woman has learnt that you don't want to make men angry. Ever.'[31] Patriarchy says men are volatile and that their anger is legitimate grounds for unleashing public violence, or just violence on the bodies of women, privately or in full view of others. Wright continues:

> Periodically, after men kill women they explain it was because the woman "made me mad." Rest assured, if anything happens to you that you do not regard as fun, and you are a woman, you will be blamed for not, somehow, making it not happen.[32]

Wright's point will be brought into stark contrast in later chapters dedicated to the Female Fear Factory in xenophobic and femicidal contexts. The lessons in patriarchal fear are not random. They form a very specific pattern designed to inculcate fear.

## Wording and Worlding

Another body of academic work on language that matters for my thinking of how fluency works in relation to the Female Fear Factory is a tradition that is conventionally taught in literary theory. For my purposes here, I will only pay attention to those aspects which are directly relevant for how language creates fear. The language philosopher J. L. Austin's highly influential theorisation of how language works not descriptively but performatively is important here. For Austin, the speech act category he calls 'illocutionary acts' is the creation of acts through language. He means that there is no reality that exists outside of language which is then merely described or transmitted through language. Instead, language is always already part of every experience. Simply put, language is inextricable to how we make – and make sense of – the world.

Although very often misunderstood as talking about 'discourse,' the point here is much more fundamental and material. Publishing in the *Journal of Pediatric Psychology*, Elizabeth O'Neal, Jodie Plumert, and Carole Peterson insist that 'language is one of the many psychological tools with which we are able to regulate behavior, structure thinking, and solve problems.'[33]

How we understand our feelings, what we think things mean, and, indeed, any human encounter is always already inside language. So, the sense of 'language' here is much more primal than what we write and/or speak. Austin takes it a little further, to underscore how language in an additional sense is an act or series of acts. Although the easiest examples of this can be found in legal language such as 'I now declare you husband and wife' in a marriage ceremony, or 'I leave my house to my sister' in a will, imagine the ways in which shouting 'slut' or 'faggot' has historically made the targeted person into that word in an actual sense. When we encounter 'I leave my house to X' in a beloved deceased person's will, that sentence is the action. It does not describe or introduce how this might be done. Upon pronouncement, the house belongs to X, and a series of bureaucratic moves are set into motion. In a less macabre setting, when a registered marriage officer mouths, 'I now declare you husband and wife,' the two people are instantly such. The words are the actions. In these instances, ownership and marriage are made.

In the case of the Female Fear Factory, patriarchy uses doublespeak to demonise women's sexuality and all homoerotic desire, to infuse words such as 'slut' and 'faggot' with similar power. Because women who enjoy sex and/or have it freely, and people who are same gender/sex attracted threaten the logic of patriarchy by fudging numerous boundaries ready-made for surveillance and punishment, the words accorded to these transgressions are very powerful. At the same time, however, it is the mere naming as such that brings danger, not only the actual desire for people of your own sex/gender. Patriarchy needs these names as stamps on those individuals who are deemed safe to violate and render outcasts. Patriarchy punishes on naming and suspicion, not on presentation of evidence of actual transgressions.

In fact, this is exactly how these words work; you are made a 'whore' or 'slut' through your being named as such, even if part of the patriarchal lie is to pretend that 'slut/whore' is descriptive. It is not. It is the making of one as such, with all the consequential power asymmetry and dangers that follow on from being marked as such. Like the legal words in the marriage ceremony and death will examples cited above, then, shouting 'slut' or 'faggot' marks the people so named as such in public.

In a society that brutalises those so named, the words become part of the signal for all fluent in the Female Fear Factory. Those so attacked recognise that being marked as such is both violence and threat. Those watching now see the attacked in the way described by the slurs. Given that people have been killed for falling into these categories, language works here to mark a target of justified ongoing and future violence.

It may or may not be interesting for readers to note that Austin's illocutionary acts were then substantially developed and vigorously feuded over by US American philosophers of language John Searle and Jacques Derrida. These developments, although eternally fascinating for me in my academic work as a literary scholar, and when I teach literary theory in postgraduate classes, are not particularly relevant for the arguments here.

## The Grammar of Female Fear

The examples above are illustrative. Below, I turn to another part of the spectrum through which fear is taught as part of being female and part of how to live as a girl and as a woman.

Former firefighter and author Caroline Paul argues that girls are taught to fear the world, and parents to 'think our daughters are more fragile, both physically and emotionally, than our sons' – but this has far-reaching consequences:

> When a girl learns that the chance of skinning her knee is an acceptable reason not to attempt the fire pole, she learns to avoid activities outside her comfort zone. Soon many situations are considered too scary, when in fact they are

> simply exhilarating and unknown. Fear becomes a go-to feminine trait, something girls are expected to feel and express at will. By the time a girl reaches her tweens no one bats an eye when she screams at the sight of an insect. When girls become women, their fear manifests as deference and timid decision-making.[34]

The connections made between gradually teaching girls to curb their curiosity about the world through the constant suggestion of danger lurking around everywhere, coupled with the lessons imbibed about girls' fragility, prime them for a life of fear. Paul's observations above are borne out by several studies on how boys and girls are socialised differently and the place of fear in socialising gender. When Barbara Morrongiello and Theresa Dawber set out to research 'Parental Influences on Toddlers' Injury-Risk Behaviour: Are Sons and Daughters Socialised Differently?' the range of ways in which their question is answered in the affirmative is both distressing and illuminating. They find that during playful risk-taking, boys are encouraged with questions on how to achieve certain playground feats, whereas girls are constantly interrupted and interfered with in the name of assistance, and explicitly.

Children are expressly told of danger in ways that suggest 'greater perceived injury vulnerability among girls than boys.'[35] Morrongiello and Dawber note how this constant interruption of girls teaches them to take fewer risks in the interest of safety. Girls are also not just 'kept safe,' they are repeatedly reminded to 'be safe,' to consider whether certain forms of play are safe. When safety becomes one of the most important considerations explicitly presented to girls, it works against the girls' confidence. O'Neal, Plumert, and Peterson are concerned with different aspects of fear and gender socialisation. However, their findings are in line with Morrongiello and Dawber's finding that 'socialising safety values in children' differs significantly across gender. Whereas teaching self-regulation of behaviour is important as children's independence increases, and 'the guidance received through social interaction becomes internalised and is available for future independent problem solving,'[36] children are offered different types of resources, and these are gendered, with girls being warned of danger at higher rates. Specifically,

> [p]arents also differed in their suggestions for children to be more careful in future, with parents being nearly four times more likely to convey this suggestion to daughters than to sons. The current findings on gender differences parallel those seen in the injury prevention literature. In particular, parents often expect and encourage boys to take more risks than girls.[37]

These repeated lessons accumulate to ensure a generally fearful outlook, especially when the dangers are generalised. Part of acquiring fluency in the Female Fear Factory, then, is for girls to be reminded that danger lurks and that they must avoid danger as a way to keep themselves safe. Conversely, boys are encouraged to take risks, sometimes to their detriment.

Importantly, this literature is concerned with what children are in the process of being socialised as. What families seek to socialise their children into often does not correspond with how the children see themselves and/or later identify as. Therefore, a child socialised as a girl but who identifies as a different gender is primed for fluency in the Female Fear Factory because this child is in the process of being made female (unsuccessfully). Under the right conditions, we acquire fluency even in languages we do not want to speak.

In her chapter 'Violence' in *Seven Necessary Sins for Women and Girls*, Mona Eltahawy writes:

> Not only are women socialized into submission, but we are told, essentially, not to be violent even as a form of self-defense but to wait until men can stop being violent towards us. When that would happen exactly is unclear and quite unrealistic,

> seeing as patriarchy has been using violence to keep us in line for centuries. We are told again and again that it is men's nature to be violent – surely that should disturb and make those men who refuse violence understand that patriarchal constructs of masculinity confine them too. We are told that women are weak, passive, emotional, submissive, etc. Which women are those things, and which women are excluded from those stereotypes? It matters because race, class, and gender all impact the ways women's violence is punished. *We have been socialized into acquiescence ostensibly for our own good.*[38] (Emphasis mine.)

Eltahawy is correct that passivity is taught to women as propriety and as a safety measure. Women are also terrorised into appearing to choose passivity. Everywhere, the apparent truth is circulated that self-defence is pointless because women – being female – are physically weaker than men – who are male, and that there is no room for variety because 'anatomy is destiny.' Yet even a cursory glance at the range of shapes and sizes human beings come in makes a mockery of this. Joan Smith reminds us that 'most differences attributed to biology, far from being innate, have to be taught.'[39]

Beyond this, she invites us to ask along with her why such beliefs and behaviours have to be taught, and why patriarchy works so hard to teach and enforce them if they are natural, if anatomy is indeed destiny.

To return to Eltahawy, because all patriarchal processes work in intersectionality with other violent hierarchies, not all women are deemed passive and weak all of the time. One of the stereotypes of African women in white supremacist society is that they are violent, quick to anger, and hypersexual. Yet, in relation to African men, we can also be defined as passive, weak, and excessively emotional. Because passivity is dictated as an appropriate response to patriarchal violence, we learn early that it is better to do nothing in order to remain safer. Although desire for safety is taught through the Female Fear Factory, real safety is elusive for women and gender fluid people in patriarchy. I return to an examination of safety in the chapter 'The False Promise of Safety.' To do nothing leaves the Female Fear Factory in place, legitimate, unchanged. Spectators are terrorised into supporting it.

## Fluency and #MeToo

In her *New York Times* piece on Harvey Weinstein's sexual harassment of her, actor Lupita Nyong'o draws on years of conditioning as a young woman across three countries, Mexico, Kenya, and the USA to mediate her increasingly harrowing experiences with the powerful Hollywood producer. She reports following the various scripts offered to women to keep themselves safe. She details a series of encounters, starting with one which took place when she was still a student at Yale School of Drama. Weinstein tries to bully her into drinking 'a vodka and diet soda' by ordering one for her even after she has refused one several times, ultimately calling her 'stubborn.' Although she is uneasy, she feigns a laugh when he calls her stubborn, something she repeats later when he calls her stubborn again, this time after she refuses his offer of a massage when she arrives at his house following an invitation to view the film there, and discovers that he has other plans. Although she writes about this evening, 'For the first time since I met him, I felt unsafe,'[40] she is careful in how she rebuffs him. Part of this carefully orchestrated avoidance of his unwanted advances is to get away safely, rather than further endanger herself.

When he calls her stubborn again, she writes, 'I agreed with an easy laugh, trying to get myself out of the situation safely.'[41] Nyong'o recalls going through a series of rationalisations to avoid naming her experiences with Weinstein violence or sexual harassment, even as she decided she 'would not be accepting any more visits to private spaces with Harvey Weinstein.'[42]

Because the lessons of the Female Fear Factory are so enduring, they require both hyper-vigilance from women and second-guessing of the knowledge of being in harm's way, despite following all the 'rules.'

Nyong'o would bring a friend to the next encounter, and then an agent. But Weinstein continued the campaign of harassment – which she characterises as increasingly crude – even after his apology at the Toronto Festival screening of her successful *Twelve Years a Slave* in 2013. About his approach to her after she wins an Oscar in 2014, she says, 'Harvey would not take no for an answer,'[43] and regarding his behaviour at the Cannes Film Festival, she remembers, 'I ran out of ways of politely saying no and so did my agent. I was so exasperated by the end that I just kept quiet.'[44] Her 'survival plan was to avoid Harvey and men like him at all costs'[45] as a way to deal with the sense of isolation she felt.

Indeed, Nyong'o mentions both fear and shame, pointing to their entanglements in how she responded to Weinstein's sexual harassment, hostility, threats, and bullying. Explaining her motivation for penning and publishing 'Speaking Out about Harvey Weinstein' in the final months of 2017, she writes, 'What I am most interested in now is combatting the shame we go through that keeps us isolated and allows for harm to continue to be done.'[46] Later in the piece, she adds, 'That's why we don't speak up – for fear of suffering twice, and for fear of being labelled and characterised by our moment of powerlessness.'[47]

These two statements are on the fear of being shamed for being treated badly, because women bear the brunt of their victimisation. Patriarchy sees women always blamed for sexual violation, for failure to act appropriately in order to avoid it, and for acting badly as a way of inviting it. In the longer narrative as mentioned above, Nyong'o performs all the dances taught to women about how to avoid violation in patriarchal societies. She smiles and feigns ease when she is made uncomfortable and in the face of masculine aggression from a very powerful man. She searches the faces of other women around him 'for any indication that she too had been made to feel uncomfortable by this powerful man' but notices nothing. Although the reason she sees nothing is likely because the other women are also feigning ease, and possibly searching her own face for the same and finding nothing, she reads the absence of evidence of other women's discomfort around Weinstein as a reason to undermine her own sense of how he acts towards her. She refuses alcohol because, already uneasy around him, she knows that alcohol may weaken her physical response time, make her more vulnerable and a quick escape more difficult. She also knows that whatever happens to her, if she consumes any alcohol, that will be used against her and as part of the arsenal to shame her.

Fear and shame isolate, as Nyong'o knows. Although dozens of Hollywood women accused Harvey Weinstein of sexual harassment, bullying, and violations of different forms, Salma Hayek was correct in drawing attention to the manner in which Weinstein kept quiet as many white women accused him of a string of atrocities, reserving his most virulent denials for accusations by two women of colour, Nyong'o and Hayek.

His responses were specifically to the piece by Nyong'o under discussion, as well as to Hayek's own 'Harvey Weinstein Is My Monster Too' in the *New York Times* (13 December 2017 edition).

## Unlearning Fluency

In her introduction to *African Sexualities: A Reader*, Sylvia Tamale writes of 'the power of language to confer power through naming and conveying meaning and nuance to sexuality concepts.'[48] In the same place, she also reminds us of the importance of feminist mapping and unmapping, which I see as tied to how she has repeatedly returned to the centrality of 'unlearning' for African feminist work. Tamale's mapping and unmapping complement, rather than oppose, each other. Mapping is important in order to get a sense of the complexities and plurality of gender and sexual expressions and encounters. Unmapping is the second stage, which emerges out of the questions posed about power on the mapped terrain.

She writes:

> Generally speaking, by the time we grow into adults many of us have done a great deal of learning, most of it rote (uncritical). Mechanical learning (cram, cram, cram, drill, drill, drill) is the norm for most of us as we move along the conveyor belt of examinations in post-colonial education systems … Both formal and informal education in the main promote learning in dualisms and absolute truths, such as right and wrong, good and bad, moral and immoral, inclusion and exclusion and male and female … The end result is that our learning processes grossly neglect to instruct us in the important concept of unlearning.[49]

What Tamale refers to here is similar to the process of attaining fluency that I have been concerned with in this chapter. She points to different ways of learning and mastering the languages and logics of domination inside and outside the classroom. As Tamale explains, unlearning is crucial to justice, to imagining freeing ways of undoing oppression, including critically engaging the logics, behaviours, and feelings we have been socialised to think of as normal. What she calls unlearning is a useful way to think about what strategies might work against the fluency that is attained in similar ways to her 'learning' as outlined in the quotation above.

Tamale's unlearning requires that we examine what fluency inculcates, that we 'discard our old eyes and acquire a new set with which to see the world. It requires us to jettison assumptions and prejudices that are so deep-seated and internalised that they have become normal and appear to be natural.'[50]

In *Decolonial Feminisms, Power and Place*, another feminist scholar, Laura Rodriguez Castro writes that unlearning also involves a specific orientation to knowledge production that obliges her to render her 'presence and epistemologies visible in the stories [she elects to] narrate.'[51] Castro's approach rhymes with my argument for rendering the Female Fear Factory strange, especially after we learn fluency, as a way to disrupt and ultimately dismantle it.

Much closer to home in terms of language is Keguro Macharia. In 'On Being Area-Studied: A Litany of Complaint,' Macharia is instructive on various aspects of how we are socialised into languages of opaqueness and validation, in ways that are exactly as I have thought of the Female Fear Factory in its initial coinage and throughout this book.

Macharia writes not on the Female Fear Factory here – although he may as well be – but nonetheless importantly, on how we might 'unlearn the fluencies' that govern and provide access. 'Unlearning the fluencies' is the process I have called 'making fluency in the Female Fear Factory strange.' In other words, what is required is not that we understand it less, or do so haltingly as people unfamiliar with it, but rather that we put the fluency to different use. To 'unlearn the fluency' is to retain the mastery but to interrupt our participation in it, to refuse to occupy the roles prescribed under it, that we know how to take up in seamless ways. Macharia links this process of unlearning the logic of these fluencies to asking questions about the 'fluencies' we need to 'give up,' in order to enter into a new conversation differently, thereby disrupting the grammar of the Female Fear Factory.

With Macharia, and on such invitation, it is also necessary to imagine different ways of creating the world, and, through 'encounters generate forms of being together unimagined and unimaginable'[52] previously, creating patriarchy-free futures.

Unlearning the fluencies is dangerous activity. It is not free of fear. Malala Yousafzai speaks of the orientation I have in mind here when she recalls her sixteen-year-old self's cocktail of determination and fear: 'I was thinking all the time that shall I put a knife under my pillow? The time was of fear, but some people can overcome fear and some people can fight fear.' And Jennifer Wright, determined to work against teaching 'girls that it's cute to be scared' remembers that as a girl, '[w]ith each triumph over fear and physical adversity, I gained confidence.'[53]

The only way to dismantle 'the factory' requires 'dangerous' feminist activity. Feminist commitment comes with the deliberate disruption of the machinery of the Female Fear Factory. Repeated deliberate and strategic interference with the manufacture of female fear leads to the eventual breakdown of parts of the machinery and eventually the collapse of the entire factory system.

# CHAPTER 3

## Dangerous Fictions

Fiction serves many purposes. Although technically an untruth, fiction echoes truth. When we encounter fiction as a creative genre, we are generally aware of it as such, but are invited to suspend our disbelief in order to fully delve into the story we are being told. This is our general experience when we pick up a short story or a novel, and when we watch a play or a film.

We immerse ourselves in the experience with a complicated combination of distance and intimacy, although we know that the unfolding tale is not real life. Our enjoyment of the unfolding tale rests on this immersion and decision to treat it as though it were real life. Appreciation of fiction occurs only when we suspend our disbelief.

As is evident in several chapters in this book, many societies work with the fiction of the patriarchal, violent man as a monstrous oddity, rather than as commonplace. This is an enduring image, despite an abundance of work showing that most sexually predatory, abusive, or rapist men are ordinary men. This powerful misconception is at the heart of why it is so hard to hold violent men accountable for their actions, and why women are seldom believed. Patriarchy casts women as liars, and it also conditions all of us to see the world through male eyes. To see the world through male eyes is not to see the world as men. It is to see the world through patriarchal legitimacy, which includes but is not limited to what Laura Mulvey termed the 'male gaze' – the sexual and objectifying visual and textual rendering of women – in her highly influential essay 'Visual Pleasure and Narrative Cinema' before developing it further in *Visual and Other Pleasures*. To see the world through male eyes also includes Mulvey's 'to be looked at-ness': the construction of women through voyeuristic lenses.

Seeing the world through male eyes is the target perspective of the world into which patriarchal societies seek to socialise us, an uneven terrain which is undermined and supported in daily individual and collective practices. A key feature in seeing the world through male eyes is the rendering of anything hostile to patriarchy as strange, abnormal, and illegitimate. When we realise that rape is *constitutive* of patriarchy – which is to say there is no patriarchy without rape – it makes sense that seeing the world through male eyes renders those who speak against rape illegitimate.

This is why the myth that rape is unusual, unintentional, and mysterious is so pervasive. If rape is all these things, then the person – almost always a woman – who says she has been raped is herself rendered strange, as are her words and the meanings she accords to things in the world. Rape victims and survivors are rendered illegitimate through unrapeability, the manufacture of female fear, and customised legal requirements that demand that they not only fall into the category of 'ideal rape victim' but also that the rapist should similarly fit the fantasy of the monstrous rapist. This is how we arrive at the notion that it is 'dangerous' for society to believe rape victims and survivors, and that rape testimony is inherently unreliable.

There is evidence of this impossible standard of proof in ordinary life as well as in numerous high-profile cases. Here, 'impossible standard' refers to the burden placed on women who report rape or speak about their sexual violation to provide irrefutable evidence in order to be believed, taken seriously, and deemed worthy of justice. Criminal justice systems across the world are notorious for denying women justice against their rapists. This requirement that rape survivors offer irrefutable proof is also a peculiarity of rape cases, which deviates from how other crimes are investigated and prosecuted.

This 'special case' status gives the appearance of recognition of the peculiarity of rape, only to have it used against those who lay charges of rape. In 'Credibility, Plausibility and Autobiographical Oral Narrative,' Jane Bennett shows that rape complainants are most likely to be believed when they meet three criteria: they experience rape in a way that leaves a particular imprint on their bodies, they fall into a category the society considers rapeable, and the rapist himself fits the profile of likely rapist as imagined by that society. There is the requirement of a body that offers evidence. Women's narratives of rape are believed based on the relationship between credibility and plausibility.

Plausibility is dependent on the listener's evaluation, but it rests on the presence of four requirements. The listener has to maintain an open mind about the events as told, consider the story's units logical, be convinced about the relationships across different parts of the story, and find the entire story believable within the listener's own understanding of societal context. Part of this context is considering the complaint believable and the accused as capable of such.

Credibility depends on how believable the speaker is. In patriarchal societies, credibility rests on whether the rape survivor is seen as a possible target of rape. When she belongs to a group catalogued as unrapeable (an enslaved woman, a Blackwoman in white supremacist societies, a sex worker), she has low credibility. To explore the ways in which credibility intersects with narratives of sexual violence by powerful men against women, I turn to two sites: one a television series, and the second the narrative of a prominent, successful Hollywood actor against an even more powerful Hollywood producer. In both cases, there are many lessons to be learnt on the construction of the figure of the violent men. In the television series, the perpetrator, Andrew Earlham, is a handsome, seemingly charming surgeon whose rape victim is his colleague's sister. In the real-life case, Salma Hayek identifies Harvey Weinstein as her monster.

Weinstein's power and substantial wealth are amassed through illusion and glamour, as well as from his ability to make and break careers in the film industry. Neither Andrew nor Weinstein resemble the myth of 'the monstrous man,' who is often cast as poor, Black or 'of colour,' unattractive, and antisocial.

Both these men are white, wealthy, friends to women powerful in their chosen careers, who are able to 'vouch' for these men's decency by their mere presence and association. If Andrew has conventional good looks and economic status, Weinstein has the seductive appeal that follows men of sizeable wealth. Both men also exhibit the characteristic arrogance that accompanies wealth and good looks, an important part of which is a sense of entitlement to women's bodies without consequence. Indeed, the dangerous fiction of powerless men as monstrous, and of socio-economically powerful men as above monstrosity, requires that we do not take seriously what 'power' means in rape, sexual violence, and bullying.

The relationship between credibility and plausibility is an unstable one. In Hayek's case, this instability of the relationship between plausibility and credibility is amplified by the fact that she is a Mexican woman. When Hayek wrote her *New York Times* op-ed discussed below, dozens of (white) women had already accused Harvey Weinstein of sexual violence of different kinds – from harassment to groping to rape. Consequently, it was plausible that there would be more accusations of the same from several other women in the film industry, given how many women Weinstein had interacted with. Rape and sexual harassment complainants are always at risk of being disbelieved.

The credibility stakes were not as straightforward in this case, however. This is because not all women are similarly constructed as credible, and their complaints as believable. There is a challenge for women who come from groups historically cast – through slavery, indenture, and colonialism – as 'impossible-to-rape' (unrapeable) because globally, white supremacy has cast white women as being in the category of those in perpetual danger of being raped, and as deserving of white patriarchal protection. Importantly, Black and Latina women have historically been constructed in ways that render their testimonies not credible. As Hayek argues in interviews subsequent to the publication of her piece, it is not an accident that Weinstein's most energetic denials of sexual violence were in response to Hayek's piece analysed in this chapter, and to Nyong'o's, analysed at length in the previous chapter.

Both these A-list actors are women drawn from groups of women constructed historically through stereotypes that render them opportunistic and hypersexual. In *Rape: A South African Nightmare,* sometime before #MeToo exploded onto the global media stage, I drew on the work of African, Latin American, and South Asian feminists to show how women from these locales had been constructed as accessible to white men through colonialism, slavery, and indenture. I used this vast archive of feminist work as the conceptual architecture for what I named the category of the 'impossible-to-rape,' which I also call the 'unrapeable.' This category comprises those whose rape has historically not been registered as violence, and who are positioned as lacking credibility in making accusations of sexual assault.

As powerful as Nyong'o and Hayek are now, they cannot escape the intersections of race and gender in these ways. More precisely, they cannot escape the stereotypical renderings of African women and Latinas. It is no accident that the two most virulent stereotypes of Latina women and of African women intersect in the stoic, excessively nurturing mother figure on the one hand, and the hypersexual being on the other. In the construction of credibility, women who belong to groups framed as hypersexual can easily be co-opted into unrapeability.

At a 2018 'Women in Motion' panel at Cannes, Hayek said, 'We are the easiest to get discredited,' referring to Weinstein's response, adding further, 'It is a well-known fact.' So Weinstein went back, attacking the two women of colour, in hopes that if he could discredit them, things could go back to what Hayek calls the 'inertia of acceptance.' In other words, then, it is no accident that Weinstein defended himself publicly against their accusations. It is not simply racist that he did so. The industry on which he built his wealth may not have inaugurated these stereotypes, because slavery, colonisation, and displacement did. However, Hollywood has fuelled and amplified these stereotypes, making a fortune as a result. This is monstrous.

The unstable nature of the relationship between credibility and plausibility is also excellently illustrated in the British television series, *Liar,* written by BAFTA-winning brothers, Harry and Jack Williams. In the series, newly single teacher Laura Nielson is set up by her doctor sister, Katy Sutcliffe, with a surgeon colleague, Andrew Earlham, whose son, Luke, is one of the students in Laura's class. The first signs of trouble are when Laura wakes up disoriented and in pain, convinced that Andrew drugged and raped her. Her response is familiar: she attempts to rid herself of any physical trace of Andrew's body and her violation. The audience recognises the bed stripping and rigorous scrubbing from elsewhere; both are intertextual references we have come to know visually from a long line of filmic representations of rape survivor responses in the immediate aftermath. The same audiences are trained in the legal requirements of a rape allegation and therefore understand that this purge also causes the destruction of any trace or DNA evidence which may assist in the successful prosecution of the rapist, Andrew.

Although Laura's sister believes her, her vaginal abrasions are inconclusive. Laura insists that memory loss notwithstanding, 'I didn't want to sleep with him.' Appearing genuinely upset, Andrew informs the expressionless detectives, 'If I thought that she didn't want to sleep with me, I would've never done it.' To further dramatise the 'mystery' of who the liar is, in a confrontation between the two in Laura's classroom, she screams, 'I said no!' to which he replies, 'No, you didn't.'

Determined to hold her rapist accountable, Laura posts on Andrew's social media page, and in the episodes that follow, there are many references to this post. Predictably, those who comment on the online thread are divided on who to believe.

The series offers excellent staging of Bennett's thesis above. Laura's credibility is questioned – not just because of her body's failure to produce the required proof of violence, but also because of her previously withdrawn charge of sexual harassment by a former school principal, Dennis Wilson. The likelihood of women experiencing more than one instance of gender-based violence notwithstanding, such pasts are often used against them, thereby decreasing their credibility.

Andrew is slowly revealed to be a serial rapist, largely through Laura's own stubborn investigation, supported by DI Vanessa Harmon, who is also later drugged and raped by him. All of this is eerie confirmation of Laura's accusation, 'You don't fool me, Andrew. Underneath the charm and expensive clothes and the I-am-just-a-single-dad act, you're just a predator.'

Laura's relentless pursuit of the truth, and her determination to find or manufacture evidence, since the truth is insufficient, does eventually lead to the reversal of the state's earlier decision not to prosecute. However, Andrew disappears, and the final episode of the first season ends with an aerial view of his lifeless body. Right up to the moment when he is found dead in the second season of the series, Andrew maintains his innocence, although, by the final episode of season one, he is rattled and asks his son, Luke, to lie and provide him with an alibi. Laura's determination is remarkable, and it is this which ultimately ensures that he will face the consequences of raping her.

The narrative arc is gripping – and Laura's stubborn will is enviable – but ultimately unrealistic. It is unrealistic because in order for the criminal justice system to finally believe her, she has to undertake extensive detective work herself, a huge task for any survivor. It is unrealistic because of the mammoth task that faces one woman – who has the time, resources, and wherewithal to fight as hard as she does – to launch a solo investigation which involves trips to other cities, all the while consistent in sufficient self-belief to persevere, despite constant obstacles and invitations to stop or pause or doubt herself. To say it is unrealistic is not to render it impossible. However, for the majority of women, the feats required of Laura are unattainable for psycho-social, economic, and other reasons.

There are several ways to interpret Laura's determination and success. First, the chances of a rapist such as Andrew being brought to book are increased by her dogged determination to hold him accountable by eschewing societal rules and legal requirements. Even though most of her elaborate attempts fail, they make for gripping television. Laura reports the rape; unmasks Andrew on social media; enters his house to look for evidence; flies to Birmingham to follow a hunch that he might have been abusive to his wife – thereby prompting her to commit suicide; buys the same date-rape drug he used on her and then uses it on him before she kidnaps him so she can stage a more believable rape scenario in an attempt to get the police to prosecute; steals his phone so she can insert spyware to track him; tracks him until she finds out where he stores incriminating evidence; hands over the flash drives that show him raping several women; and, ultimately, kills him.

It is a fictional genre, and therefore not meant to correlate with real life, as long as it is believable. However, audiences cannot help but make connections between the fictional world portrayed and the real world it resembles. This is especially so given how brilliantly the series captures aspects of real-life rape culture: the expectation of the monster rapist, the inadequacy of the criminal justice system in dealing with how rape usually happens, how isolating rape is, and the constant fear. For, although Laura stands up to Andrew at every turn, what is hidden from him, but always revealed to the viewer, is how frightened she is of him, even as she tells him she is not. Each phone call and encounter with him rattles her. Even when he is not around, she battles to sleep, and struggles to keep her life together. Everything is affected, including her teaching. Therefore, it is clear that she pursues him in spite of the constant fear. She tells a therapist that while she does not care about herself, she cares about creating consequences for him. To a potential new friend, she admits that rape has broken her.

She may have levels of stubbornness that are superhuman, but her success is not heroic triumph over fear. It is a daily confrontation of a fear that she will not be flattened by. This is a hopeful vision.

A second interpretation is one many engaged in the fight against rape already know: that the justice system very rarely provides justice for rape survivors. By design, it will fail more than it succeeds. Therefore, any chance of success requires an almost unhinged determination to work outside this system.

After all, when Laura reports the crime, even though DI Vanessa Harmon and DS Rory Maxwell, the primary investigating detectives, believe her, the decision to prosecute goes against their recommendation.

This second reading is supported by the third: Laura is only able to prove Andrew's culpability because he is a serial rapist who records each attack. The presence of two other women he has raped does not advance the case at all, even when one of these women is DI Vanessa Harmon, whose rape is superfluous because she believes Laura and works hard to find evidence even prior to Andrew raping her. It also adds nothing to the narrative arc, except to add her wife, Jennifer, to the long list of suspects for Andrew's murder. In other words, Laura can create legal consequences only because Andrew is both a serial rapist and a voyeur.

The series offers a consistent critique of rape culture and of the image of the monster rapist by showing how romance and shame are implicated in the creation and fortification of the Female Fear Factory. The series also performs some of what it critiques through the obsession with irrefutable evidence. When Laura drugs and kidnaps Andrew to create a rape that more closely resembles the mythical one required by the criminal justice system for the purposes of prosecution, this is a clear indictment of the system as unjust. Her real rape has no chance of being taken seriously, but a false one might. She finds the requisite evidence that will make sense to the police and courts, and will be sufficient for a conviction, as DS Rory Maxwell confirms in the final episode. However, it does not matter, because Laura will kill Andrew before he is arrested in any event, after she has worked so hard to find irrefutable evidence of his guilt. The first season subverts the terms and demand for legal evidence – only to re-instate them in the end.

There is a fourth reading, which did not occur to me as I watched the series and wrote the first draft of this chapter. Laura's case shows the inadequacy of the system to bring Andrew to book, to create consequences for him.

## Monstrosity and Power

In her powerfully named *New York Times* opinion piece, 'Harvey Weinstein Is My Monster Too,' Salma Hayek details her nightmarish series of encounters with one of Hollywood's most powerful men, Harvey Weinstein.

In March 2018, she would later tell Oprah Winfrey in a *Super Soul Sunday* interview that she was less concerned about what exactly would happen to Weinstein than the importance of not looking away from a problem that is systemic. She insisted, 'We are taking conscience of a problem we looked away from,' and this is consequential for gender in the industry as a whole. Her use of the word 'conscience' here is also telling. The honesty about gendered and other forms of violence in the television and film industry (and beyond) is important. This is the 'Me Too' movement that Tarana Burke started, to make visible the widespread use of sexual violence across institutions and parts of society, to create a connection between sexual violence, fear, and interventions to interrupt it. Burke did so many years before Alyssa Milano made it a hashtag, #MeToo, on whose back Burke's movement travelled. Whereas the face of #MeToo quickly became the powerful white women who importantly spoke up, it is important to note the ways in which it did not confer the same levels of visibility and/or credibility to all women who spoke out, even among the powerful. More importantly, here, is Hayek's insistence on systemic attention to the problem rather than mere individuals who must bear the cost of conscience and other costs. However, the consequences of conscience have to be collective to retain it as a movement in the manner of Burke.

In the same interview, Hayek expresses both shame at not having spoken out sooner and feeling like 'my pain was so small' –

when more than seventy women had spoken out. She adds that she had told herself that 'there's no point for me to talk because it just happens to everyone, you know? And then I felt by itself, it was just my own little drama.'

In her opinion piece, Hayek points to her uncertainty about the implications of speaking out, her subsequent politeness towards someone who had been so violent towards her, her regret at not telling her loved ones about the assault sooner, and whether or not it was her friendship with two prominent men that had 'saved' her from getting raped. She had approached Weinstein with her dream film project, *Frida*, on the iconic Frida Kahlo, while she still considered herself a 'nobody,' something which Weinstein would confirm to her repeatedly.

When he agreed to make the film with her, Hayek writes of how this became the beginning of a time where she had to repeatedly say 'no' – to his stalking of her; to his repeated requests for her involvement in different sexual acts; to his increasingly bizarre requests for showers and massages involving other people in different roles. Hayek writes about how 'with every refusal came Harvey's Machiavellian rage,' to the point where she even had her life threatened by him.

His sexual advances, demands, and threats of violence were widespread, as the entire world would eventually find out. However, at the time, Hayek felt isolated and torn because she was making a film she had worked hard to have made, and one she would not risk being cancelled. These harrowing conditions were never acknowledged, even after the film he had tried so hard to sabotage (both during its filming and afterwards) was not only a hit, but also garnered multiple Oscar nominations, and two wins, including for Hayek's leading role.

Writing of persisting, despite Weinstein's reign of terror and his constant degradation of her, she surmises, 'In his eyes, I was not an artist. I wasn't even a person. I was a thing: not a nobody, but a body.' Her position as a first-time producer, and as an actor, who had star status in the Mexican television soap opera world but had not yet become a big name in Hollywood, opened her up to this additional vulnerability. This isolation, as well as her sense of sexual harassment and bullying as commonplace, contributed to her fear of speaking publicly about Weinstein even as her star began to rise.

Indeed, Hayek says she would smile and be polite to him and try to remember other aspects of their interaction, thinking all the while of dealing with his increasing bullying as 'telling myself that I went to war and I won.'[54]

Real-life monster Harvey Weinstein and fictional monster Andrew Earlham understand the permission and benefit of the doubt granted to powerful men in their societies, under the cover of the Female Fear Factory. Their victims also understand the monumental task of being believed, knowing that the violence targeted at them is widespread, but also that those who speak about their violation are more than likely to be shamed and punished.

The two examples in this chapter offer two very different enactments of the dangerous fiction of the monstrous violent man. Rather than being easily discernible, showing obvious signs of monstrosity, he hides in plain view.

# CHAPTER 4

# Mythologising Misogyny

Although it is now nearly a decade since news of the Delhi bus rape came to world attention, the details remain with many of us. On 16 December 2012, returning from watching a film with a friend in celebration of her recent graduation, twenty-three-year-old Jyoti Singh was gang-raped by six men on a bus and her companion beaten up, as the driver continued to drive on, signalling his apparent support for the violence unfolding on his vehicle. Singh and her friend were then thrown off the bus. Because Indian law does not allow the naming of a rape complainant in the press, she was given the name 'Nirbhaya,' meaning 'the fearless one.' This is a fascinating choice of a name, which both romanticises and obscures the fear that Singh must have felt, a move that erases her experience even as it renders it hypervisible and useful. I use her name here because her family subsequently insisted that her name be used after her death in hospital on 29 December of the same year, suggesting that this was in line with her wishes.

As previously discussed, the language, names, and stories that societies tell about gender power and crises are not innocent. While it goes without saying that some rape cases will receive more attention than others, it is important to note that studying such prominent cases often illuminates a society's anxieties about gender power and women's lives, on the one hand, and the systems through which value and fear circulate.

The cases that make the headlines are all instructive: there is no safety. In 2019, high-profile cases included a twenty-seven-year-old veterinarian who was raped and killed, a four-year-old who was raped by a neighbour, and a six-year-old who was kidnapped and raped in North India.

Jyoti Singh's experience drew international media attention, not because rape is a rare occurrence in India – the rapes that make headlines and, in many instances, are reported to the police, represent a fragment of the total rapes in any one country. Singh's case drew attention because of a combination of factors, including the identities and social positions of the violated and the perpetrators, and the peculiar sequence of events in this particular case. It was a moment that politicised many women in what Kaur (quoting Wertheim) calls a 'feminaissance': 'an urban creative-critical rising with women at the fore,'[55] and suggests that part of the anger was linked to the fact that the men who raped her were also men of a lower caste.

For an undoubtedly complicated combination of contextual and competing motivations, the case galvanised actions. Many rape cases draw national media attention in India, a country in which some statistics suggest that roughly ninety rapes are reported per day to the police. Other recent high-profile rape cases that hit the media include Kuldeep Singh Sengar, a former legislator from the ruling Bharatiya Janata Party (BJP) who was convicted of raping a seventeen-year-old in 2017. Due to police inaction, the survivor attempted to set herself on fire, while her father was arrested and beaten in custody for repeating his daughter's accusation.

The events of this case are important for the manufacture of female fear. First, there is the presence of a really powerful man in the state apparatus at the very centre of the violence, as perpetrator. In the unlikely event that people uncritically associate the law with justice, and power over the law with commitment to fairness, here is one case that spectacularly explodes such associations. Not only is a man, entrusted with the setting up and maintenance of a key regulatory system for an entire society and state, here caught showing the system reckless disregard, but the response of other parts of the state come to his aid, rather than to that of the young woman he has raped. The young woman's frustration over the failure of the police to deal with the case is so pronounced that she considers killing herself, by setting herself on fire – itself a highly loaded way for women to die in India. Across the world, women complain of how the police drag their feet, how slow the legal system is, how seldom justice lies within the criminal system for survivors of gender-based violence. So entrenched is the entitlement to women's bodies that naming it is understood as a challenge, and resisting it is met with further patriarchal reinforcement – violence.

The jailing and beating of this father for insisting on justice for his daughter – something owed to her by the police and state – becomes not just a site of state brutality against another citizen but another site for the manufacture of female fear.

All rape is both a message and the fulfilment of the threat of violence. It is not a moment, but the language of the Female Fear Factory.

Of Nirbhaya's six rapists, one was a minor who was released after three years, one died in prison, and the other four were hanged in prison in March 2020.

Ironically, one of the measures through which the Indian state communicates its purported opposition to gender-based violence is through a very high-profile 'protect your daughter campaign.' The image of the imprisoned and beaten father is a sharp reminder of how farcical this campaign is. The campaign's name also betrays another reason why it cannot signal what it claims. To call on parents, and specifically fathers, to act the role of protector is to admit the state's inability to meet its obligation of providing security to its citizens. Therefore, this campaign's wording is counterproductive. It does not mitigate violence against women by men, but re-inscribes masculine power as legitimate. It is very clear communication of the state's unwillingness to keep daughters safe. It is a staging of patriarchal disregard: the invitation for individual men to take on a task that the state is incapable of delivering, one that is too big for the state. More worryingly, this is the manufacture of female fear. Daughters are fluent in this register, and will need little assistance decoding the threat at its heart.

'Protect your daughter' is sinister, spectacular foregrounding of the power of the Female Fear Factory. Rather than addressing the source of the fear in order to eliminate it, it legitimises a protectionist, infantilising masculinity. But this doublespeak, which is present everywhere in patriarchal society, can often be found in those cast as well-meaning allies.

In his book, *Courting Injustice: The Nirbhaya Case and Its Aftermath,* Rajesh Talwar, as lawyer and legal scholar, spends considerable time asserting his opposition to gender-based violence, as well as virtue-signalling through the many conversations he has with other Indian lawyers about the inadequacies of the Indian legal system when confronted with gender-based violence cases. He is sure to point out that some of these lawyers are now presiding officers in their own courts – able to set case precedent. Yet, this collective exasperation is difficult to understand. For, if lawyers and judges are unable to make the law work to better meet the ends of justice, or to work to create a legal framework that meets the requirements which Rajesh Talwar claims are desired by the legal fraternity, then what is the point of seeking legal recourse? It must have been the question the seventeen-year-old raped by a legislator asked herself during the trial, and the one that must have preoccupied her when she almost set herself on fire the following year as her father lay brutalised by the very same state apparatus which had shouted 'Protect your daughter!' at him.

There is a degree of special treatment with which high-profile cases are treated, and Kaur notes that:

> [t]he various elements of the Nirbhaya effect may be located along the following spectrum ranging from memorialisation, affirmative solidarity, ironic provocations, rescripting the master narrative, and somewhat at a tangent, sensationalisation.[56]

The Nirbhaya effect is used by various writers to refer to responses to the gang rape's movement into the arena of public awareness, the shock expressed by large numbers of Indian people, as well as the many organised protests that were unleashed across different Indian locales as a result.

Jyoti Singh had to be named something in order for activism and discussions to take shape on her behalf. At one level, her naming as Nirbhaya was an attempt to fix a certain set of events in relation to her in the public imagination, to give her a face. Her memorialisation starts with keeping her memory and the specific events of her rape and death in the public awareness. The specific name given to her is also telling. It is the name of a goddess, an attempt to return power to her when she enters public consciousness through a violently disempowering evening. The name, which I will return to later in this chapter, keeps her alive in the imagination of different collectives who are moved by what was done to her. This goddess name is an attempt to claim her as worthy of memory and recognition, a strategy that runs counter to the actions of her rapists and the bus driver that fateful evening.

A memorial is a memory aid and a political act of recognition that someone is important and powerful. It is therefore no accident that the name allocated to her is one that defies the fear that she must have felt, and the fear that retelling her narrative evokes in the hearts of many listening women. Yet, other meanings leak from this engagement with fear. Rather than elevating Singh to the realm of the deity and heroic, couching her ordeal and courage as fearless communicates two patriarchal messages.

First, it obscures the experience of the same woman it seeks to elevate. Second, like the performance of public violence, it reminds many others that it could have happened to them, and that it still could. The entrance onto a bus for many other young women (and men) who had not questioned such an act in these particular ways previously also becomes another mundane activity which they now need to approach with vigilance. Paradoxically, then, naming her as fearless highlights and aids the Female Fear Factory, rather than undoing it.

The Nirbhaya effect does not inaugurate the Female Fear Factory in the Indian context. As in other hierarchical and patriarchal societies, women and other marginal groups have a keen sense of their own victimisation and vulnerability, even if this effect partly invites them not to feel fear. This includes the manufacture of female fear through famous and less iconic cases. However, the famous cases have additional impact, not just those memorialised, like Jyoti Singh's, but also those of the powerful men mentioned earlier in this chapter as part of the context of India's mediated rape cases.

Paying attention to Talwar's language on the Nirbhaya case reveals deep patriarchal investment. He refers to the case in ways that set it apart as an 'especially troubling case,'[57] to Jyoti Singh as a 'twenty-three-year-old girl,'[58] and to the case itself as one involving a sequence of events involving 'brutality beyond belief,'[59] even though, by his own admission, he has seen many rape cases.

The Female Fear Factory thrives under conditions in which rapes are placed on a continuum. Rape culture depends on the framing of some rapes as mild and others as especially shocking and/or brutal. To label any rape as particularly brutal marks some rapes as mild. Yet, rape is by definition brutal. Rape culture depends on this classification.

Perhaps then, it is when we examine the evidence in his study, and his chosen tools, that we are able to understand the exasperation experienced by Talwar and his colleagues. It is clear that the many years of exposure to rape cases has not assisted him, and neither did the 2019 sexual harassment charges against the Chief Justice of India (CJI), Rajab Gogoi, invite any faith in the judiciary's stated commitment to fighting gender-based violence. The fact that the accuser in the 2019 case rejected out of hand the composition and methodology of the panel convened to deliberate and adjudicate on her complaint further clarifies how deeply ensconced the manufacture of female fear is in the bosom of the Indian state and legal systems.

The Nirbhaya case provoked mass outcry, detailed by Ahmed, Jaidka, and Cho thus:

> The news was widely discussed and debated in traditional and social media platforms; the latter became a hotbed of public agitation and indignation, which ultimately went off-line, to the streets, as mass demonstrations and protests.[60]

Mass outcry led to the establishment of a judicial committee and the passing of the Criminal Law (Amendment) Ordinance in 2013, followed by other new laws and the establishment of six fast-track courts for rape cases. Although there is an increase in public attention to matters of rape, the legal system remains slow in its administration of justice.

In addition to the activism online and on the streets, the case has inspired an outpouring of artistic responses. Inchley reads a play, inspired by the rape, Yaël Farber's *Nirbhaya*, which stages 'testimonies of violence against women' for audiences by performing a shift from the testimonial to the persuasive. These fictionalised testimonies serve as context that assists audiences to make sense of the Nirbhaya rape, not as an isolated and exceptional instance, but as commonplace violence. This is an important gesture, because we understand patriarchal violence better when we position ourselves to observe the emerging patterns.

However, the shift from testimony to attempts to persuade audiences troubles Inchley, in execution and in structure. She argues that although the play moves from the premise of women's experiences of rape as being at once specific and shared across a range of sites, how these are put to use in the larger creative performance is problematic. Rather than occupying spaces as important points of reflection and provocation, they are reduced to functionality. This elevation of practical political argument oversimplifies and does injustice to the value brought by witnessing as creative mode. Instead, this rich site is sacrificed in order to render the narrated experiences more audible. For Inchley, the appropriate word is 'sacrifice.' The prioritisation of audibility of women's struggles ultimately displaces women's voices by locating them in the realm of strategic intervention for political mobilisation.

The challenge raised by Inchley here brought to mind the work of two African feminists who have repeatedly revisited the difficult boundaries between silence and voice. For Nthabiseng Motsemme, the elevation of testimony and speech often occludes other sites of meaning. These meanings are embedded in forms of 'muteness' which, although easily mistaken for silence, are nonetheless powerful signifiers. In other words, there is meaning in the mute. It is not the site of absence. Indeed, for Motsemme, the elevation of speech can be at the expense of uncovering richer, more layered meanings, structures, and possibilities.

Importantly then, for Motsemme, the generative response to muteness is a tentative approach rather than aggressive mining for meaning. It is a questioning, cautious approach that reveals the layers of meaning in the mute, as well as in the provisional, punctuating silences.

So, how does Motsemme speak to both Inchley's dissatisfaction and Farber's project? The witness testimonies speak loudly enough on their own, and have the ability to generate meaning and transformative analysis without needing to be processed into explicit political motivation. Leaving testimonies without clear strategic use is more than symbolic. It is a different performance of power, one that avoids the nub of Inchley's unhappiness: the displacement of women's voices in a play that begins by staging women's testimonies of rape.

The second framework comes from filmmaker Xoliswa Sithole and is the conceptual vocabulary of 'the shouting silent,' which she develops in a film of the same name. The shouting silent is not Motsemme's mute, even if it is similarly impractical. The shouting silent has demands on how we focalise. It is invested in excavating what surfaces when the world is read from the least empowered position in a situation. In other words, instead of the rush to conversation, strategy, and questions, orientation towards the shouting silent requires that we retune our ears to a different frequency. Audibility requires repackaging for easier, clearer consumption.

## Unmasking the Ordinary Rapist

Deepa Mehta's 2016 filmic response to the Nirbhaya case takes off from the knowledge of the words on screen in the opening scene: 'No one becomes who they are in isolation.' In the film, *Anatomy of Violence,* she is concerned with making sense of the specific combinations of patriarchy, misogyny, poverty, and class that produce the specific kind of violent men, like the ones who raped Jyoti Singh. As she told audiences at the 2016 Toronto Film Festival and India Film Festival Canada, while she grasps that misogyny and patriarchal violence produces 'monster' men like these in every society, that men who act like this respect no national boundaries, she wanted to see the conditions of their production. She was clearly dissatisfied with the framing of these men as exceptional monsters, when global gender-based violence statistics clearly point to their 'Anyman' (rather than Everyman) status. On platforms after screenings of her film, she also shared the response she had received from many men after previous screenings. Individually, men had walked up to her to discuss the film, determinedly opposed to gender-based violence and patriarchal oppression in their introductions to her, perplexed as to why she wanted to humanise the perpetrators.

Sometimes this humanisation opened her up to accusations that she had rendered violent men sympathetically. Mehta's representational choices are fascinating to me because I share her impatience with the portrayals of rapists as exceptional, monster men. In *Rape: A South African Nightmare*, I insist that although women are still pressured and/or shamed to 'break the silence,' come forward and report, there is no silence about who the targets of the Female Fear Factory and rape culture are. What there is a silence about – and this silence enables rape culture – is who the rapist is. It is not enough to say he is everywhere just because this is true. It feels inadequate to say we all know a rapist or several because otherwise the statistics make no sense. I had insisted that we break that silence by asking to see the face of the rapist.

I read Mehta's project in a similar vein, but as an attempt to understand the rapist's context, not in order to deprioritise the victim or survivor, but in order to illuminate something which seems key to the production of rape culture. By now we have accumulated substantial material on the production of femaleness, and in this book, I take a magnifying glass to the machinations of the Female Fear Factory. What is just as important to understand are the specific ways in which patriarchy *makes* rapists.

We know the general contexts and conditions of their making, but the precise ingredient of the explosive cocktail that Mehta's film seeks to analyse is a dimension I am also curious about. Because I do not invest too much time studying men, however, it is a curiosity I can engage only obliquely, even if not marginally.

At the same time, the case of how ordinary rape is, and the face of Anyman, would strike very close to home for me. After I had published a book on ending rape wherein I had issued many calls – one of which was to unmask the rapists who do not necessarily get reported, in order for us to be able to create the costs that I also insisted needed to be urgently crafted – a surprise awaited me too. An artist friend, whom I had always imagined to be embattled about his own sexuality due to an aspect of childhood trauma, was outed as a serial rapist. I had made this assumption about his sexuality based on dimensions of childhood trauma that he had shared with me in previous years.

I mention my former friend's unmasking because we had spent considerable time discussing and being angered by endemic misogyny, gender-based violence, and homophobia. This same friend had previously terminated a friendship with someone because he had been accused and found guilty of sexual harassment. In other words, despite many encounters with violent men at work and elsewhere, and a history of involvement in organisations and university processes that dealt with rape and sexual harassment, nothing in a decade of friendship with this man ever gave me pause.

As painful as this particular discovery was, I am even more convinced of the need to create a cost for perpetrators of patriarchal violence that goes beyond, alongside of, and in spite of, the legal justice system. This is why Mehta's project and her haunting questions are so intriguing to me. Mehta goes beyond the call to name and identify the rapists in order to understand the making of rapists so that as feminists, we can better know how to disrupt that process as part of our work to end rape.

There are more dimensions to the makings and motivations of Anyman. One of the nagging questions for me in the rape of Jyoti Singh is the status of the bus driver who continued to drive all over the city while a woman was gang-raped on his bus and a man beaten; a bus driver who eventually slowed down or stopped long enough for both victims to be thrown off the bus.

## Facing Fear

Sneha Rajaram makes several additional interventions in analysing meanings ascribed to aspects of the afterlives of Nirbhaya's rape:

> Despite being in a world of pain, Jyoti Singh gave a full statement to the police. That takes courage, yes. But what if we have taken that amazing show of courage too far? What if the name 'Nirbhaya' doesn't allow her to be human in our eyes, doesn't allow her to be scared? She had a right to be scared if she wanted to [sic]. Would we respect her less if she had been scared, even for a moment, during the painful

> medical procedures she went through? Or is the very thought blasphemy?[61]

Rajaram is aware of how Jyoti Singh became Nirbhaya: because of the need to provide a name for someone who could not be named at that point, for legal reasons. For Rajaram, even the best intentions and practical considerations should not prevent interrogation of consequences. Indeed, she insists that there are difficult questions about the continued resistance to using Singh's real name after her permission and death. While according her a name was an attempt to make her real to a public that did not know her, while respecting the limitations posed by the law, the name has significant implications for her humanisation. Being given a goddess's name, rendered fearless, also places her outside of the realm of the human and relatable.

She must have been afraid. Therefore, what does the celebration of the absence of fear do to her memory? These are important questions.

Rajaram insists on a way to imagine a courageous woman who was still afraid, of reckoning with the power of fear as real. When women are placed in the realm of goddesses, it can be difficult to imagine them as human and fallible. The placing of women who have been brutalised in the realm of the non-human – deity or myth – is also a gesture of recuperation, an attempt to render them whole again, beyond the realm of the human. But recuperation and mythologisation rarely serve women well.

The intention to elevate and heal Singh is noble enough. However, to the extent that she suffered what real women are subjected to daily – not goddesses and mythological figures who can transcend human pain and fear – after Rajaram, we have to ask, again: what does all of this mean as an engagement with the Female Fear Factory? As Rajaram argues, we need to reflect on this 'processing' of Jyoti Singh by 'turning her into a goddess,' a familiar trope that does not apply only to her, because this deification has implications.

In a linked manner, Nisha Susan has also previously argued against this insistence on talking about ordinary women as goddesses in her critique of a battered woman campaign that relied on the same trope. There, Susan had argued that Save the Children's 'Save our Sisters' campaign against domestic violence dangerously sets up an imaginary audience of the 'general public,' which seems to speak neither to the abused women nor to their abusers in Indian society. The deification of women survivors makes it similarly difficult to imagine a perpetrator, even when specific perpetrators are known. This creation of a 'general public' is not something exclusive to India. In South African non-feminist campaigns against gender-based violence, the viewing public is often framed as though composed of people from another country, even as we live in a country with high statistics of every form of gender-based violence, a country where the majority of the viewing public is likely to be constituted of survivors and perpetrators. This stance enables the continued circulation of campaigns that are doomed to fail, targeted as they are at imaginary audiences.

Not mincing her words, Susan calls the overly used slogan 'enough is enough' (which is everywhere in South Africa too, along with 'never again') 'one of the emptiest and smuggest slogans in human history.'[62] She is correct about the waste and human cost of campaigns and slogans which are popular but have design flaws that render them ineffective in the fight against the Female Fear Factory, rape culture, or any other aspect of patriarchy. Such statements, like campaigns that ignore the society they are meant to work in, leave unaddressed the many concentric circles of complicity, averted gaze, and victim blaming.

Painfully, Sneha Rajaram further asks whether this deification of brutalised women is because 'a goddess or daughter/sister is the only kind of woman (or rape victim) we can respect.'[63]

While this chapter has focused specifically on a high-profile Indian case, it is instructive beyond the site of origin. As patriarchy mutates, which it must do to retain its power, it infiltrates aspects of oppositional discourse too. This should be unsurprising, given that Gayatri Chakravorty Spivak has long reminded us of the ways in which oppressive systems stay alive by infiltrating and hijacking the language of liberation movements. As is clear from Jyoti Singh's case, and with echoes to other locales, the names we offer to rape complainants in rape cases that capture the public imagination matter.

# CHAPTER 5

## The False Promise of Safety

Patriarchy runs on fear: fear of being an outsider, fear of being brutalised, fear of being too much, too inadequate, too vocal, or too different. It requires hard work to avoid being an outsider in a patriarchal society, because it is a system that relies interchangeably on oversimplifying and exaggerating the construction of gender and sexual categories. As a result, the categories are easily ill-fitting at best and suffocating at worst.

Yet, the cost of being 'too different' from the dictates of your own gender prison is meeting with violence. Too much deviation from the script of the feminine or masculine, and/or from compulsory heterosexuality comes with a price that ranges from shame and ostracisation to death. Patriarchal fear is so pervasive that it shapes the seemingly banal choices we make about body styling, jogging routes, times to be out in public, and where we feel free to go alone. This is because fear is an excellent way to keep people under control because it forces us to police ourselves, in the false hope that we may be able to keep ourselves safe.

In 'South African Women Live with the Burden of Constant Vigilance,' Koketso Moeti recalls her own fear when she had to allow men to fix an electricity fault in her home, and as they departed, she felt remorse. She writes:

> Quietly I got a knife and kept it close by. They eventually fixed the problem and I felt bad for suspecting the technicians of wanting to harm me.
>
> And yet, as most women know, my fears were not unfounded. The latest verified data shows that a woman is murdered every three hours in South Africa, a rate which

> is almost five times higher than the global average. Add to that the grim reality [of] recent police statistics which show a 4.6% increase in reports of social offences, which also include rape and sexual assault, and I know my reaction was justified.[64]

This excerpt is telling in a variety of ways. Despite myths that typecast certain groups of men as more likely to be violent, the high numbers make it clear that while not every man chooses to violate women, there are no reliable cues that enable women to tell the violent ones from those who are not. Furthermore, in a country with the statistics that South Africa has, women live in this state of 'constant vigilance' that Moeti so clearly illustrates here and elsewhere in her writing.

This heightened vigilance requires that women consider how they will fight back, or modify their behaviour, to try and remain safe. Many women adopt a combination of these strategies as they go through their days. To grasp at safety, they often have recourse to a range of scripts that hold out the false hope, and false promise, of safety.

However, even this false hope of safety is a con. It is a hope sometimes offered to us as a promise, if we comply with patriarchal gender scripts and perform the expected roles, by staying in place. To be female is always already too much, which is why female fear has to be manufactured in theatrical and banal ways to lock us in place. But oppressive systems are nothing without mythology. We are taught to imagine we can escape. This false hope or promise of safety – and therefore freedom – is tattooed on our very skin and psyche as we are taught to inhabit patriarchal gender identities.

The promise of safety demands self-policing. It requires what bell hooks has called 'an antagonistic relationship with myself' when you are a woman. For women in South Africa, as elsewhere, it is increasingly clear that the scripts we inherit on how to minimise the likelihood of being targets of violence are a con. There is no safety, only the dull awareness of the possibility of safety perpetually deferred. From childhood, girls are taught to bear the burden of responsibility for a system designed to cut us down individually at best, or annihilate us all at worst.

Scripts are repeatedly handed to us as part of the performance of the false promise of safety. These scripts, like much of patriarchy's toolkit, appear to be about ensuring our safety and minimising our risk, whereas by design they achieve something quite apart from this. Their promise is more than just false. It is menacing in three interrelated ways.

First, these scripts are presented to us as though our very existence as women depends on them. If we deviate, we will be placing ourselves in danger, and so as we acquire fluency in them, we police ourselves, limit our own freedoms in order to grasp at that transient or elusive safety. When we give in to our desires for freedom and improvise, and in that process of casting aside the script, someone violates us, it is our deviation that is responsible. Sufficient fluency means that it is our fault that we get beaten, abducted, trafficked, groped, raped, maimed, and killed. Entire legal and religious systems are trotted out to establish the facts of our exact deviation – and fault.

Second, these scripts ensure that we become agents and enforcers of patriarchy against ourselves since we are presented with two options: safety through compliance, or violence. They take on a commonsensical appearance and turn us against our own interest. In other words, although the scripts are presented as hopeful, they are part of the system of keeping us fearful. For to adhere to the script is to lock us into a pattern of fear, and a life of fear. The script is part of the apparatus of the Female Fear Factory. Patriarchy cannot remain whole without it.

The third menacing aspect lies in the extension of this 'commonsensical' dimension that the scripts take on, once we have become so fluent that we police ourselves as the default way of living our lives. Imagining it as a way to protect us, we then sometimes partake in instructing others in the same oppressive language. We pass it on to those we feel protective of, imagining that we are keeping them safe from the fear, when we are actually passing it on, infecting them with the same.

In 'Sitting like a Girl', a chapter in *Reflecting Rogue: Inside the Mind of a Feminist,* I narrate the story of how my maternal grandmother constantly policed the ways in which I enjoyed sitting or otherwise contorting my body as a girl. I hated being instructed to adjust my body to postures deemed more decent, but we did not have the kind of relationship where I could have openly challenged Nkgono. I took comfort in the knowledge that she visited only several times a year and would return to her own home soon enough. Thereafter I would resume openly sitting how I liked. My parents did not seem to care how I sat.

My grandmother and I never had the conversation, but in that essay I imagined that she unintentionally passed on fear to me, intending to do the opposite. I was a wilful child, and, as a defiant woman herself, but also a woman of her generation, she was keenly aware of the multitude of dangers that could befall a Blackgirl in apartheid South Africa. She was trying to offer a buffer. But this is exactly how fear is passed on within and across generations.

But what are these scripts?

## Script One

*Dress like a good, respectable girl so that you can be chosen as a proper wife and earn respect by association. Dress this way so you do not look like a despicable woman who enjoys sex and who may or may not use sex to make money.*

This script divides women into two kinds: the good ones and the whores. The good ones can be discerned through their clothes and behaviour, which means they will eventually be chosen – and rewarded through marriage to a man. Script One posits compulsory heterosexuality as reward rather than prison. Respectable life choices and sacrifice are cast as respectable and valued femininity. Beyond this, respectable and desirable femininity has its opposite.

Any woman can be made into a whore. A woman can be constructed as a whore as long as there is evidence of wilfulness. Such wilfulness need not even directly find sexual expression. Indeed, any woman who has had sex, or enjoys sex, or makes a living from selling sex, is in danger of being categorised as 'a whore.' To be a whore is to be safe to violate and cast aside.

The fear of being a whore is so significant that girls and women are cautioned against all manner of joys if by participating in them they can be read as whores. They are required to adjust their clothing, the amount of make-up they wear, where they meet their friends, and any manner of desired body-styling and life choice to avoid being called a whore.

Whores are the women whom patriarchy says are safe to violate, and at the same time whose violation is deserved punishment for defying gender and sexuality classification systems. I have previously shown how some women are rendered as whores in order for the legal justification of their institutionalised and routine rape. The case of The Slave Lodge in Cape Town is a good example. The Slave Lodge – where enslaved women were kept before sale, in between transfer, when recaptured, or when they were considered the property of the Dutch East India Company (DEIC) – is a good example. The Slave Lodge was also often labelled the Cape's first brothel in slavocratic South Africa from the seventeenth to the nineteenth centuries.

Script One says whores are unsafe, whereas respectable, good women are safe. It stops short of pointing out how easy it is to be a whore when you are an adult woman who has had a sexual past, as Pregs Govender[65] pointed out about Fezeka Kuzwayo, the complainant, during the rape trial of Jacob Zuma in 2006. Script One wants us to assume that girls will have enough time to grow into adult women in order to be classifiable as good or bad women.

Yet, as journalist and feminist writer Gail Smith wrote during the Zuma trial, South Africa is 'a society that does not sufficiently protect or respect its women and girls.'[66] Such a script makes no allowance for the reality that on 24 September 2018, a twenty-two-year-old white man would follow a seven-year-old Blackgirl into a women's toilet cubicle at Dros, a family chain restaurant in Pretoria, and rape her. In a trial that made headline news and also sparked a debate about the different treatment of white versus Black accused rapists, Nicholas Ninow was revealed to have threatened both the child and those who discovered the rape with further violence.

The script requires that girls and women assume that an adulthood will be reached without encountering the likes of Bob Hewitt, Wimbledon champion, whose case I spent considerable time on in *Rape*. Hewitt was entrusted with coaching and training several girls who had aspirations of tennis careers in the 1980s and 1990s in South Africa. He was convicted of raping girls by a high court in Johannesburg after three of his now-adult victims fought to see him brought to book.

Script One would have you assume there will be no Nicholas Ninow to follow you, a seven-year-old girl, into the bathroom stall of a family restaurant, or a Bob Hewitt to molest you when all you want is to excel at tennis by learning from a Wimbledon champion.

This script leaves out the fact that, a year later, now eight, the survivor may have to relive it all and testify against Ninow for a legal system whose definition of justice needs not recognise that re-traumatisation can persist for a lifetime, even if a perpetrator admits guilt and goes to jail. It omits that one of the three adult survivors finds out after the fact that Hewitt is up for parole, when the parole board has consulted none of the adults who were the children he raped. Olivia Jasriel, one of the three, told Johannesburg-based SAfm radio show host Stephen Grootes that the entire ordeal was 'just a constant re-rape,' and as she did so, her words echoed in so many survivors' hearts on 16 September 2018.

The first script insists that safety under patriarchy is ensured if girls remain good and grow up to be good girls, because good girls will be deemed worthy of a husband who will then protect them and keep them safe from patriarchy. As the examples above show, and there are millions more beyond, the problems with Script One start long before girls even grow up enough to become adults. Children of all genders are terrorised and brutalised long before they can reach adulthood, so the assurances of Script One are deferred. This is to say nothing of the fact that little girls do not always grow up to be women, and women who want to be wives.

There are other scripts.

### Script Two

*Do not head out after dark and, if you do, ask men you know to walk with you. Men you know will keep you safe from bad, strange men, the legitimate owners of all public spaces. If you can, stay in the wealthier parts of town, where there are fewer bad strangers.*

Script Two omits that bad men are not all strangers, as Moeti reminded us earlier in this chapter, and as many survivors of gender-based violence know. Sometimes the bad men are the ones you choose to love as friends, family, or partners, because there is no foolproof detection technology. The second script is silent on the ones who walk into or break into your house and kill you.

No one warns you that if your name is Anene Booysen, a teenager who was raped and disembowelled one night, that the script is a con. Nothing in the script suggests that it is possible that on a Saturday morning, 2 February 2013, three months after Anene turned seventeen, she would die from her severe injuries.

Anene followed the script to the letter. Having gone out, she did not venture too far away from her working-class neighbourhood of Bredasdorp, but went to Kallie's Pub, a social space frequented by many people she and her siblings had grown up around. When she was tired, she was aware of the Female Fear Factory, and, following this script, she agreed to let only very specific men escort her home. She had been warned all her life that as a girl she should not venture outside in the dark alone, that she should not trust strangers, but insist on being accompanied by a known, reliable man. She knew the men she asked to walk her home well, because they were her brother's classmates. Yet it was these very men who raped her, broke her fingers, cut her throat, beat her face and disembowelled her, before leaving her for dead. Her broken body was discovered by a security guard where it had been dumped just hours before. Anene died in Tygerberg Hospital, but had told her foster mother that Johannes Kana was responsible for her fate.

The second script is silent about the fact that if your name is Uyinene Mrwetyana, an undergraduate student at the prestigious University of Cape Town, walking into a post office in the Southern Suburbs of Cape Town on a Saturday afternoon, 24 August 2019, excited about receiving a package, you may be raped and murdered by a post office employee.

Luyanda Botha had planned the rape and murder of Uyinene, which is why he made her come back at a different time to collect her parcel. The Clareinch post office is on a busy road in a middle-class suburb, next to a police station and opposite a school. Even with the vigilance with which South African women walk around, nineteen-year-old Uyinene could not have feared being raped and killed at a post office. Botha recounted in his statement prior to sentencing that Uyinene had put up significant resistance, fighting him off so vociferously that he had realised that the only way to overcome her was to bludgeon her with a weighted scale that was within his reach. It was the heaviest thing he could find. His chilling exact formulation rendered in his (and Uyinene's) mother tongue underscored that she 'had given him a very hard time'[67] and 'had taken very long to die.'

In public discussions about precarity in South Africa, it is commonplace to mention the various ways in which gender power is indelibly shaped by class and race. When carelessly rendered, these discussions suggest that middle class women are safe. Uyinene's case shows the difficulty of such a claim, because neither the private school and elite university education her parents could afford her, nor her residence in a secure university residence in an affluent suburb, could protect her against a late afternoon attack by a post office worker. She could be raped and killed with the police next door unaware and therefore unable to intervene.

Indeed, Uyinene Mrwetyana was the embodiment of the kind of young person South Africa likes to hold up as the future. By all accounts, she was brilliant, feisty, and kind. She was also unapologetic in her contempt for patriarchy and relentless in her questioning of obligatory heterosexuality.

Jesse Hess, a theology student at the University of the Western Cape in Bellville, Cape Town, and her eighty-five-year-old grandfather, Chris Lategan, with whom she lived, were found murdered on 30 August 2019. Her body was discovered on the bed, while her grandfather was found tied up in the toilet. A television, cellular phones, and a backpack had been taken. One of the two suspects in the ongoing case is a close relative of theirs who is also linked to the rape of a sixteen-year-old in a different part of the city. Her aunt, Natasha Hess, revealed that the accused had been jailed in 2007 for raping a family member, and had been released only in December 2018. She also spoke of how terrified nineteen-year-old Jesse had been of this man.

A long time ago, I heard Lebogang Mashile say in an interview – the specifics of which I no longer remember – that South Africa habitually produces the kind of woman it also habitually annihilates. And the tens of thousands that came out in a massive expression of pain and rage in the aftermath of the murders of Uyinene Mrwetyana and Jesse Hess, and too many others – who were overwhelmingly young women – recognise the truth of what Mashile said in that interview. They recognise whose blood regularly runs down the streets of this and other countries. And like many women of their generation in marches around the globe, and previous generations of radical South African women who made the apartheid state and their male comrades quiver, they will not lie down and die. As several of the #AmINext marchers in Cape Town said in viral video footage, 'They may kill us, but we will die fighting hard.'

Adhering to this second script does not help you, because you can still be killed in a public institution during the day, or in your own bed at home.

## Script Three

*Stay in school so that you are not dependent on a man. When he starts to act in ways that make you uncomfortable, unsafe, or he outright abuses you, leave. If you do not leave, then he will get worse. Get out with your life, and make sure the police know.*

This script is a kicker because it has some basis in truth, because patriarchal financial control is long-lasting. Financial dependency and abuse are easier to escape from when there are other available options for a full life without the abusive partner. However, many kinds of abuse happen regardless of the financial status of the partners. It is not true that independent financials cancel out the effects of other forms of abuse. Nor is abuse always immediately recognised as such. Obligatory heterosexuality means that all over the world, children are groomed for the perfect patriarchal romance, domesticity, and control. In many contemporary societies, romance is paraded as an intoxicating cocktail of choice and chance. Obligatory heterosexuality also teaches women to desire domination, whilst framing such domination as natural, regardless of financial means.

Much goes into the kind of ideal person that should be chosen as a lover. Love is work, we are reminded constantly. It is compromise and passion and unpredictability. If you choose well, there are always elements of chance and disappointment. Patriarchal romance glamourizes domination and violence, recasting them as energising passion.

Patriarchal societies romanticise control and abuse by men in heterosexual relationships as commitment, real love, or simply 'going through a rough patch.' What about the fact that Thobeka Maqashalala, a doctor, was stabbed and drowned by the scientist husband she had known all her life because she wanted to leave him? Or another doctor who was recently shot in the head by the husband she had left, as she was trying to collect a few belongings from their home? He did not let their children's presence in the house stop him as he killed her.

This script did nothing to save these women. It offers little consolation for you, if the man you are in the process of divorcing kills all four of your children, the same children he looks so protective over and loving towards in family photos. These are the details of just one of many cases constantly in the South African press.

## Script Four

*Learn to fight so that you know both how to defend yourself effectively and how to inflict the most harm on a man's body. This will keep you safe. It surprises and unnerves men when women know how to fight, especially when those women know how to fight well. Women also need to know how to use legal means to protect themselves. Report violence and get protection orders. Go to the police for help. Real violated women report.*

For many women, and for one whose name is Leighandre 'Baby Lee' Jegels, this script about protecting yourself is particularly cruel. A black-belt karate champion for four uninterrupted years, she was a superior fighter. She was skilled, measured, composed. When this same woman became an undefeated boxing champion, not only was she obviously a star athlete, but she also entered a level of skillset rarely achieved. Add to this busy international athletic career a degree in science education from the University of Fort Hare, and it is clear just what a remarkable twenty-five-year-old she was.

But Baby Lee's black belt and boxing gloves could not stop the three bullets fired at her from her ex-boyfriend's gun, nor the one he reserved for her mother, Rita. The protection order against her police officer ex should have led to the confiscation of his gun. Baby Lee was a fighter who used her hands, her fists, her mind, and the courts to fight. She could protect neither herself nor her mother the last Friday of August 2019. Patriarchal violence won against a woman previously undefeated.

It bears repeating: Baby Lee was an outstanding fighter and tactician. A violent police officer ex-boyfriend's sense of entitlement to her life, his arrogance in believing that the laws he is sworn to enforce do not apply to him, the knowledge that he would physically lose against her saw her bleed out next to her car on the side of the freeway in the city in which I live. As a Tactical Task Team officer, Bulelani Manyakama knew how to plan the shooting and get away, as he was apprehended in a hired car over two hundred kilometres from the scene. He had been involved in a car accident, killing a further two people that day – a nurse and a librarian who were in the other car. He would die from injuries sustained in this accident a few days later.

Jesse Hess and Baby Lee were murdered on the same day, a week to the day after Uyinene Mrwetyana's own murder. The two first-year university students were nineteen, while the star athlete graduate was twenty-five. They could have contributed so much to the world. All three cases, extensively covered in the media, were high profile. Because Uyinene had first made the news because she was missing, the news of the murders of these women hit the national headlines at the same time. It felt like there was a killing spree of women across the country. This is because there is. There were many other cases of women targeted for violence in the news at the same time, and many more that did not make the news. If it felt like there was a war against women in South Africa that week, it is because there is.

Four scripts. Women raised in patriarchal societies know these well. We also know that there are more, and none of them keep us safe. Instead, they exhaust us and kill us. They require constant work and vigilance and they still do not work. In addition to the lie of 'safety' constantly dangled ahead of us, which we know is elusive, but which we are socialised to pursue, there is another sinister dimension. Knowing the magnitude and scale of what we are up against because it is paraded daily is not enough for patriarchal control. When women constantly modify their behaviour in pursuit of the unattainable safety, they take on the responsibility of what misogyny creates. Women are held responsible for their safety.

We have to refuse this burdensome responsibility and fight for a safe world for all of us. Walking wounded as many of us are, we are fighters. Patriarchy may terrorise and brutalise us, but we will not give up the fight. As we repeatedly take to the streets, defying the fear in spectacular and in seemingly insignificant ways, we defend ourselves and speak in our own name.

# CHAPTER 6

# Femicidal Intimacy

El Salvador is to femicide as South Africa is to rape.

El Salvador and South Africa are seldom mentioned in the same breath. The histories of their constitutions could not be more different. Where they are remarkably similar is in their formative histories. Both are nations forged through multiple regimes of violence that have rendered violence as vernacular. As with any language, dialects abound, which means that these societies have highly differentiated inflected forms of violence, each contributing differently to commonplace violence. In 1992 and 1994 respectively, El Salvador and South Africa were coming out of eras during which violence had been so sedimented that they would need Truth Commissions to assist the two countries to heal and make sense of the transition.

Both Truth Commissions yielded more by way of amnesty than prosecutions. This institutionalisation and large-scale performance of amnesty created something: forms of knowledge about the permissibility of violence – and the old logics of violence as legitimate. More on this below.

In her book on traditions of Black feminist writing under apartheid, *And Wrote My Story Anyway: Black South African Women's Novels as Feminism,* Barbara Boswell illuminates how consequential the exclusion of rape, and all forms of 'gender-based violence' from the definitions of both 'torture' and 'human rights violations' in the Truth and Reconciliation Commission (TRC) founding documents was. She shows that it was more than a travesty and an omission. Regardless of where one stands on the successes or failures of the TRC, it defined parameters of the unacceptable in the South Africa it was shaping. In other words, if we think about the TRC as part of the machinery through which a new South Africa, or post-apartheid South Africa, could be built, it also clearly drew the boundaries of (un)acceptability. It was one of many missed opportunities we continue to pay dearly for. In this regard too, we share not just the decade of great transitions with El Salvador, but the cost of these missed opportunities.

Both Truth Commissions offered very little by way of prosecution and were excessively generous when it came to amnesty. These missed opportunities, exclusions, and failures are implicated in the continuities shared between apartheid and its aftermath in South Africa, and the US-sponsored three-decade civil war and contemporary El Salvador. The failures to deal with the compounded trauma of the El Salvador population reeling from the civil war, built on successive military coups, sitting on centuries of colonialism and its contestations, is implicated in the continuing availability of violence as spectacle and as vernacular in that country.

In this chapter, I discuss femicide through the stories of two women born and raised in countries on opposite sides of the globe. But these are not deadly stories rendered useful. I juxtapose them because they offer much to teach and remind us about misogyny's patterns and gestures. Both cases attracted media attention and created additional media effects. The stories of violence against women that draw mass public attention have much to teach us about the ones that go unreported. In *El Salvador: The Story of Karla Turcios*, Patricia Sulbarán Lovera simultaneously points to the ruling violence of her society and the ways in which private and public spaces are equally immersed in violence. She says hers is a country that has too long prioritised violence as a way to resolve conflict. This, too, resonates – even if the names we give to the violent masculinities that hold women hostage in both societies differ.

The story in this chapter is one of two young women, each killed by the men they had chosen to share their lives with. When I read about the award-winning journalist from El Salvador who had been killed by her husband, I was struck by how familiarly odd this man's behaviour was. The story of how men kill women whom they claim to love is an old one. And we are all fluent in the language of deadly heterosexuality, but when I read of Karla's murder, I thought of Karabo Mokoena, even though there had been more recent devastating manifestations in the news.

I have chosen these two stories here as much for their similarities as for how they differ. Desensitised to the South African statistics, albeit not what they portrayed, I was reminded of the importance of numbers in the telling of a story when I read that eighty percent of femicides in El Salvador go unpunished. I am rarely shocked, but seeing this number repeatedly, a new number for me, revealed something I had long taken for granted about why the criminal system fails women in cases of rape. I may not expect gender justice to come from the police and law courts, but I still believed something about how they worked, prior to my encounter with this statistic. Many cases of rape and battery disintegrate on the requirement of evidence. If dead women are not evidence of femicide, what is?

In *Femicide in South Africa*, Nechama Brodie addresses this fallacy of bodies of evidence as being straightforward by tracing a range of inadequacies in police collection, coupled with the unreliability of numbers, since people often obscure cause of death in numerous ways.

Most femicides and intimate partner violence is not reported to the police. This has not changed even with a slew of new laws and structures, such as the women's courts, introduced in 2012, with judges only dedicated to gender-based violence cases. The gap between the books, on the one hand, and survivor/victim experiences, on the other, is several oceans wide.

Hospitals are the source feminists and other researchers turn to for a sense of scale in El Salvador, but more on that later. When economic journalist Karla Turcios was killed by the man she shared a life, a home, and a three-year-old son with on 14 April 2018, hers was the one-hundred-and-fifty-second femicide case of 2018. You read that right. In mid-April, she joined one-hundred-and-fifty-one women who had been killed for being women in her country.

Brodie reminds us of the importance of distinguishing between female homicide and femicide, even if she later subverts this distinction. Using the work of Diana Russell, who coined the term 'femicide' in the 1970s to refer to the killing of women for being women – whereas female homicide includes all killings of women – Brodie nonetheless makes a compelling case for reading female homicides as femicides under patriarchy. The cases analysed in this chapter are femicides in the Russell definition.

When Turcios did not immediately respond to the usual morning text, on Saturday, 14 April 2018, her mother noticed and found it strange. By the time her son called later that day to say his sister was missing, she knew something was wrong. Karla's body was found two days later, on Monday, 16 April, barefoot and with two plastic bags over her head. Mario Huezo, her husband, had driven an hour and a half away from their home to dump her body on the side of the road. The story he would tell about his whereabouts would be contradicted by the police cameras that had caught him twelve times, and the seven private-citizen cameras, on the freeway from San Salvador to Santa Rosa Guachopilín, on the Saturday she disappeared. In their evidence to the 'specialist gender judge-only court,' which they also shared with journalist Sulbarán Lovera, the police would argue he was on his way to and from the dump site.

After Karabo Mokoena died, her boyfriend of a few months, Sandile Mantsoe left their flat to drive to two places. First, he drove up the road to get petrol. Then he drove to his mother's house in a different part of the city to get a car tyre and pool acid. Returning with these items, he loaded the woman he had been in a relationship with into his car and drove her to a deserted spot, positioned her with the tyre around her body, doused her in pool acid and petrol and then set her alight before walking off. He reportedly related this story to the police in a calm and detached tone. When Mokoena's mother had called to check on her daughter, whose phone remained unanswered, Mantsoe had told her he was unsure of Mokoena's whereabouts, but – bizarrely – had assured her he had not killed her daughter.

This must have been a strange statement about a woman who had not been missing long enough even for a police report to have been issued. Perhaps because of the frequency with which femicide is reported in the media, Mokoena's mother did not take the talk of her daughter's death at face value. By the time of Mantsoe's trial, however, recalling the casual delivery of that statement must have been devastating for her.

Huezo and Mantsoe mechanically disposed of the bodies belonging to Turcios and Mokoena as though they were nothing. There is a disturbing level of ease that is suggested by the specific steps the murderers chose. Driving with the dead women's bodies in their cars, they were confident enough to drive long distances, in order to place further distance between themselves and the women they had recently been intimate with.

Mantsoe had additional convictions added to his sentence for deliberately trying to mislead the police and obstruct the course of justice. He had come up with all manner of lies to create an impression of Mokoena as unstable that could not stand up to scrutiny, including a narrative of events that required the assistance of the security officials in his block of flats. When approached for verification during the investigation, as well as on the witness stand, security officers from his building denied any involvement in his stories; no camera footage collaborated his claims; and the incident log books remained free of any mention of the elaborate stories he had made up for the police and law court. It seems strange that he had the presence of mind to drive all over Johannesburg, buying and collecting what he needed to burn and dump Mokoena's body, but lacked the matching cunning to make up a convincing story to cover his tracks.

The two men are similar in this way. Perhaps the arrogance of successfully disposing of the women's bodies gave them false confidence that their respective attempts at cover-ups had been effective. They are also similar in terms of the detail of the killing of these two women.

Huezo maintains his innocence even from the jail where he will spend the next fifty years of his life. He also frames himself as a victim because of his gender. In an interview with journalist and author Patricia Sulbarán Lovera, he makes many excuses and insists that Turcios's case received all this attention because of the fact that she was a journalist, all the while speaking about himself in the third person. He claims journalists are interested in this story because the victim was one of their own, and would be dispassionate had she been in a different profession. Clearly resenting all this attention, he repeats that if the roles had been reversed, his case would not have received as much attention as it has.

He is also oddly determined to write a book about this crime, even though he claims to know nothing about it save for what he discovered from the investigation. His frustration clearly stems from how he ended up in jail after the care he took to dispose of his wife and her phone at separate points along the route, far away from their home. To kill a woman in a country that is the world leader in femicide, where reporting of such a crime is highly unlikely, and still end up with a fifty-year sentence, must be puzzling to him.

Mantsoe appears less affected by his sentencing. He maintains that Mokoena committed suicide and that he simply disposed of her body, which was burnt so thoroughly that an autopsy could not determine the cause of death. During sentencing, the judge called him a 'devil in disguise,' as he singled out for special mention the lack of any signs of remorse from Mantsoe during the duration of the trial. The judge is certain that this man is a danger to society.

There is no shortage of strange details which emerged during Mantsoe's trial. Having taken such care to ensure that Mokoena's body was burnt beyond recognition, he took the police to the scene of the crime and shared his disposal methodology. An estranged wife with two of his three children were also a revelation during the trial. The third child was with a former lover, Nonhlanhla Dlamini, who claimed he had left her for Mokoena.

It is very clear how immersed in various registers of violence both these men are. They demonstrated fluency both in violence as enacted in the home and in mastery of its concealment. And both were terrible storytellers, which is how they were caught. Comfortably positioned within highly circulating violent practices protected by machismo and other violent masculinities, they both had reasonable chances of escaping punishment. They both seemed confident they would.

One of the incredible insights from Patricia Sulbarán Lovera's report is how she traces the impact of the Karla Turcios case on journalistic conversations and praxis in El Salvador. This case has brought home to journalists the reality of the extent of violence in their society. She shows evidence that the aftermath of Turcios's murder has been used as an opportunity to reflect on how journalistic conventions enhance the possibility of change and justice, or whether the language of reporting is complicit with existing structures of violence in El Salvador. In other words, Turcios's death has challenged the people in her profession to reflect deeper about the ethics of reporting on gender-based violence – and violence more broadly.

Clear from Patricia Sulbarán Lovera's report is that there is pervasive reluctance to report gender violence to the police. This is partly due to the lack of faith in the likelihood of justice from the legal system, as well as cynicism informed by constant reports of violence from the police themselves. This fear of reporting is the reason those doctors and hospitals interviewed had a higher number of cases than the police force, which, in any event, only has a twenty percent success rate. This means that the small percentage of Salvadorians who do report gender-based violence to the police have a higher possibility of experiencing more crime from the police themselves than they do of getting a conviction for the criminal. Medical staff show that only one in six survivors treated for domestic violence lay a criminal charge with the police; they also report knowing the trends so well that they can sometimes predict when patients who have stopped coming have died. A single hospital showed Sulbarán Lovera that they had already treated thirty of the victims in the cases that ended up as femicide, by the same April during which Turcios was killed.

These numbers point to women's fear and reluctance to report cases to the police because of lack of confidence in such machinery. Furthermore, cultures of machismo and violent masculinities find easy circulation in societies where violence and fear are commonplace and are part of the socio-political landscape. Huezo's shock at being caught speaks to his awareness of the safety of violators in his society. Even with the best chance of escape from successful prosecution for femicide in the world, Huezo was caught and sentenced on 31 January 2020. This was the end of a fast nine-day trial more than eighteen months after the death of Karla Turcios.

With similar odds, Mantsoe was sentenced on 3 May 2018 – almost a year after the murder. Addressing Mantsoe at sentencing, high court judge Peet Johnson said:

> In sentencing you the intention is not only to punish you for what you have done but also to serve as a warning to others that this type of conduct, and I am stressing this kind of abusive conduct towards women, is not to be tolerated in our society.[68]

Here was a senior officer of the law demonstrating a very different position from that espoused by his colleagues quoted in legal scholar Rajesh Talwar's book, discussed in 'Mythologising Misogyny,' earlier in this book. Where Talwar and his friends simultaneously spoke of the inadequacies of the legal system in dealing decisively with gendered violence and chose not to use their own positions as powerful jurists to intervene, Judge Johnson not only exercises his power but understands the symbolic effects of his judgement in challenging public perceptions about the permissibility of the abuse and terrorisation of women.

Karabo Mokoena and Karla Turcios lost their lives too soon and under horrifying conditions. There are many aspects of the Female Fear Factory's operation and disruption that are at play here.

These were real women, but their cases also work to create symbolic meanings. The attention they attracted – and the successful apprehension and prosecution of both men – communicated meaning and possibilities to more than those directly affected by their crimes. These famous cases are also similar to many cases of femicide across the world. Both women were murdered by men with whom they were in romantic relationships and who killed them in their own homes, underscoring how dangerous many homes are. The calculated ways in which these men then disposed of the bodies of the women they had just killed illustrates another dimension of patriarchy's successful dehumanisation of women even – or perhaps especially – under conditions of patriarchal romance. There is a cold, calculated precision in how both men felt safe enough to transport women they had just killed across large distances, with no fear of being interfered with. This contrasts sharply with women's occupation of public spaces. Because these men's relationships to public space are so direct and comfortable, they felt certain that they could accomplish their missions without fear of detection. This is in sharp contrast to women, whose movement in public is policed, commented on, problematised and otherwise interfered with regularly, in a multitude of ways, some of which are discussed in the opening chapters – 'Manufacturing of Female Fear' and 'Fear, Fluency, and Control' – of this book.

Equally striking was the way in which both men tried to obscure something about the women's bodies. This seems to be about more than the mere disposal of the bodies. Two plastic bags are tellingly placed over Turcios's head, and therefore obscure her face, rendering her obliteration complete. It is a very dramatic expression of erasure because once her face is bracketed away, she could be nobody, any woman. For Mantsoe, the end of the encounter comes once the match is struck. He does not wait because he is certain that he has brought together the proper combination of substances and items to get the job done. His dissociation from her is complete when the fire takes. He is so successful at distancing himself that even an experienced jurist comments on this at sentencing.

These men are fluent in the registers of violence circulating in their societies. Huezo may not be a member of a cartel or other organised crime syndicate, but he is fluent enough in their work – because of the high circulation of this violence in public – as well as in discursive circulation in his society, that he can replicate these modes of violence. A phone randomly tossed off the side of the freeway will not easily be linked to the body of the woman it belongs to. A phone will be found and then be linked to organised criminal activity, and therefore will not warrant very different interest. Mantsoe chooses to enact a particularly graphic mode of violence associated with those deemed sell-outs under apartheid. To be a sell-out was to be a Black person who sided with white supremacists against other Black people and the freedom project. Although there was always the possibility that the person accused of collaborating with the apartheid state was innocent, because misinformation was rife as one of the state's deliberate tactics to control, in the public imagination the detection of spies and sell-outs was constructed as a simple, stable process.

Necklacing was the subject of much contestation in Black counterpublics under apartheid, but it also had support, partly because of the fear of what it meant for anyone to be seen as defending a spy. Presumably, the possibility of being set alight alive with a car tyre and petrol would also be a more frightening deterrent against working with the state. Mantsoe's choice of obliterating violence is curious for further reasons. Necklacing was highly visible, but neither a frequent occurrence nor one with a long public life, with the first two such incidents occurring in March and June 1985 respectively, and the final one reportedly in 1991. Mantsoe's age suggests that he was born either in 1990 or 1991 and was therefore not raised in a South Africa where this form of public killing was available as a register. It is as strange as the setting on fire of Ernesto Nhamuave, which I mention in a later chapter, 'Foreign Familiars,' of this book. It is clear that the public, routine performance of violence creates regimes of meaning that are difficult to undo. Although these two men have no direct link to the groups whose forms of violence they rely on to dispose of the bodies of their partners, these registers of violence are sufficiently accessible to them so as to be rendered useful.

The specific uses of violence in these public cases communicated to broad publics, and to journalists, in very specific ways. Patricia Sulbarán Lovera begins her report on the murder of Karla Turcios by eschewing objective distance, opting to create a link when she declares that she too is a Latin American journalist. This self-positioning points to her own vulnerability at the same time as fortifying her position of authority – as a journalist and as an insider to the culture. Both the vulnerability and the authority come with important insights. From this position, she is able to both sensitively cover the story with nuance, and offer a powerful critique of the culture that provided the contexts for Karla Turcios dying as she did.

These intersecting positions are harnessed when she stands between two powerful male symbols that are everywhere in Latin America: revolutionary heroes and religious figures. In a public square, she stands between statues erected to celebrate religion and a war hero, to make the point that 'religion and violence are the pillars of this society.' Signs, and the ways in which public space is organised, matter to render some things possible and others not.

Signs matter. They are not just statues.

Indeed, Lovera's highlighting of these signs rhymes with Rachel Pain's insistence in 'Space, Sexual Violence and Social Control' that 'spatial patterns are central to descriptions and explanations of women's fear,' as well as her claim that

> [w]hile it is not true that all women share the same experience of fear of crime, broad trends exist which suggest

> that women's fear is significantly different from men's fear. The spatial patterns of women's perceptions of risks, of the actual risks they are exposed to and of their behavioural responses have implications for their equal participation in society.[69]

These stories do not only speak to El Salvador and South Africa, however. From the UK, long before these deaths, Joan Smith writes of being a journalist covering a serial killer, Peter Sutcliffe, dubbed 'The Yorkshire Ripper' (even though two of his women victims were from Manchester). Smith's journalism in the late 1970s is another world away. Yet, there are strong echoes with the concerns already grappled with in this chapter.

First, she writes about an encounter with the police officers working the case in her book, *Misogynies*:

> I was sent to a police press conference where I interviewed George Oldfield, head of the West Yorkshire detective team known as the Ripper Squad, and was dismayed by his masculine bluster … As yet, any lack of confidence in him was unformed, built on little more than a fleeting impression.[70]

Later in the chapter, it becomes clear that her first impressions were very important. These same detectives are the reason it took so long to catch the Yorkshire Ripper. More accurately, the specific forms of white patriarchal perspective they brought to the case continued to place larger numbers of women in danger, rather than interrupting and apprehending the serial killer. This is due to the value judgements they made about the lives of some of the earliest victims. These judgements were not evaluated, but taken as valid with no clear basis in anything other than patriarchal policing of women. One of the key attributes in the construction of the serial killer's victim profile was that of a 'prostitute.' Two of the victims were women the Ripper Squad allocated to the category of 'whore,' which they then officially designated as 'prostitute.' I have already discussed in an earlier chapter that all women are always in danger of being constructed as whores. They are either good women (such as mothers and virgins) or bad women (whores). Women who trouble the boundaries of patriarchy are often marked and/or treated as whores.

Two victims were made into whores by the Ripper Squad. One was a married woman who enjoyed an outing with her women friends one night a week. This inappropriate behaviour of being out in public after dark, and doing so regularly for pleasure, fell outside of the ambit of appropriate female behaviour as far as the Ripper Squad was concerned, and so she became 'whore.' It was not difficult to move from 'whore' to 'prostitute.' The second woman was similarly challenging to the Ripper Squad because she had been in a relationship with a Black man.

Historically, white men constructed and institutionalised Black sexuality as excessive and bestial. There was an already existing construction of white women as delicate and the property of white men. These two collided to position Black men as that from which white women most needed to be protected. The virtue of white women depended on it. To be a white woman who desired and formed relationships with Black men was to be a whore. Therefore, accessing this old white supremacist patriarchal archive, the Ripper Squad marked this second victim as 'whore' too.

It was this violent patriarchal fantasy which was responsible for endangering several other women's lives. Women are made whores in order to justify their violation. By constructing these women as whores, the detectives symbolically enacted on them what the Yorkshire Ripper had played out on their bodies. And, thus, Joan Smith convincingly demonstrates that although the Ripper Squad repeatedly assured the public that their killer profile was so accurate that they would be able to identify the Yorkshire Ripper on sight, they interviewed him several times without even realising it, and released him to kill again. They had created a fantasy man who was a monster version of themselves, and therefore missed him because he was an ordinary version of themselves.

With an inaccurate profile, Joan Smith informs us, they included a woman killed by someone else but who herself could easily be made into a whore, and missed two actual victims whom they did not immediately know how to make into whores. This is why it was the work of the South Yorkshire Police, as opposed to that of the Ripper Squad detectives, which led to the successful arrest and conviction of the Yorkshire Ripper.

Clearly, UK circa 1975-1980 and contemporary El Salvador and South Africa are not the same, nor can they easily be collapsed into one another. Nonetheless, each of these sites shows something about the trap of male certainty, the predictability of arrogant masculinity across different patriarchal societies, whether or not the ruling masculinities are paraded as machismo, violent masculinities militarised.

The radically different position of the detective who solves Turcios's murder case and the question of the successful disposal of her body is due to the fact that she has a different vantage point, which allows her to crack the case. Such a position can be engendered by a lifetime of being gendered in harmful ways or it can be cultivated, as in the case of the presiding officer in Mokoena's case. In the Turcios case, witnesses kept informing the detective of how perfect the relationship between Huezo and Turcios was, since they were always together. Where others saw romance, she saw the classic warning signs of a controlling man and an abuser, pursued that line of investigation, and uncovered an abusive, femicidal Huezo.

There is a second echo:

> Like other women working at the radio station, I was constantly aware of my dual role of reporter and potential victim; by day I reported the latest developments in the story, by night I could not sleep when I returned to the Manchester suburb where I lived alone.[71]

Smith's position here rhymes with Lovera's – to produce a productive interplay between vulnerability and insight gained from insider status – and also finds resonance in the courageous undercover journalism by Mordi and her colleagues, discussed in my chapter 'Bodies of Knowledge,' later in this book. As a woman, she feels vulnerable because there is a known serial killer about. The irony here is that those trusted with catching the Yorkshire Ripper jeopardise their own case, whereas a young woman reporter has a much better sense of who the Ripper might harm. This clarity is even more pronounced now that we know that two of his victims came from Manchester.

Juxtaposing men from three different societies, located in nations that do not lend themselves to ready comparison, illuminates the ways in which patriarchy's violent patterns can be glimpsed across the world. In chapter 2, I discussed the fluency which women and others who have been made female – or who are in the process of being constructed as female – acquire in the Female Fear Factory. In many ways, this chapter is a counterpoint to that one, demonstrating the extent to which fluency in violent masculinities and other aspects of the Female Fear Factory emboldens men to further endanger women.

# CHAPTER 7

# Bodies of Knowledge

In many contemporary societies around the world, there is a deference accorded to science, scholarship, and academic universities that often assumes that intellectual pursuit is not mired in the ugly matters of sexual violence. This has often struck me as simultaneously oddly ahistorical and inattentive to current patterns of what periodically appears as institutional culture at universities across the world. While it is true that universities are not always in the news for sexual violence, there are occasional glimpses from what makes the news, whether the universities are in North America, Asia, or your own country.

Perhaps it is because many of us read the news as a chronicle of moments, as presented in a news cycle, before we move on to the next thing. This orientation to 'moments' is particularly well-suited to obscuring sexual violence, which presents patterns as individual encounters.

It strikes me as ahistorical because, rather than being separate, universities and the knowledge we produce in them are deeply implicated in institutionalising sexual violence. The academy is mired in regimes of misogyny and sexual violence, as many academic feminists have repeatedly shown. Zine Magubane's work has revisited these connections between disciplines and sexual difference and violence in various guises: in her work that shows how colonial science weighed and measured women's brains to make arguments about capacity, intellect, and social place, as well as in her scholarship on colonial Britain and South Africa.

In other work, she has probed how a specific trajectory of post-structuralist discourse actually re-inscribes Sarah Baartman as 'Hottentot Venus' while ostensibly theorising against racism and patriarchy in what Magubane calls a 'curious theoretical odyssey.' Yvette Abrahams's historiography on Baartman, but also on the obsession of various European scientists with measuring Khoi genitalia in the nineteenth century in the name of science, and the search for the missing link between ape and humans though various bodies of southern African peoples, also highlight the ways in which sexual violence has a long history of use in the academy in the name of science.

Similarly, South African journalist Gail Smith had been horrified to discover the remaining jars in the Musée de l'Homme in Paris, filled with the pickled brains and genitalia of Native American/Amerindian, Asian, and African people collected as part of the joint enterprise between science and colonial extraction. George Cuvier, fêted anatomist and memorialised as one of the most pre-eminent European scientists of all time, could, with the greatest self-satisfaction write, 'I had the honour of presenting to the Academy, the genitals of this woman, prepared in such a way, that leaves no doubt on the nature of her apron.' This 'apron' was one of the manufactured reasons so many southern African women were probed and prodded. This Cuvier, Gail Smith reminds us in her essay 'Fetching Saartje,'

> was not just any old scientist. He was the best of the best, a respected surgeon who counted Napoleon amongst his patients, and a man obsessed with human anatomy and the secrets it held about different races.[72]

Walking through the Musée de l'Homme as part of the film crew that went to film the repatriation of Sarah Baartman's remains, Smith is struck by the bodies collected in the name of science, rows of cupboards carefully catalogued with pages that 'listed the contents … skeletons, skulls and other bits of indigenous people from every corner of the earth, but mostly Africa, North and South America.'[73]

If this is how Native American/Amerindian and African women enter the realm of European science, is it any wonder that this preoccupation with chopping young women into pieces continues? What is more, beyond the women of the African and American continents, much feminist scholarship exists on the persistence of linking women's thinking with their reproductive organs and hormones, whether in the Freudian hysterectomies as treatment for depression, or in other gruesome collusions between psychology, psychiatry, anatomy, and gynaecology.

I outline all of this to briefly show that the current academy is built on the intersections of empire and misogyny in the construction of the disciplines. There are many more lines that connect these processes, but such retracing can be glimpsed elsewhere in my own other feminist scholarship. I have a different task here, for which the above is background.

The connections between sexual violence and scientific knowledge are not limited to the university. They permeate other spaces of knowledge creation where women's contribution is codified as the entrance of already sexually available bodies. This history of entering science and the academy through genitalia, hysteria, measured brains, and scrutinised labia is in the very fabric of the contemporary university's institutional culture.

It is only very recently that women were allowed entry into universities for scholarly pursuit as students, and even more recently, as teachers and researchers themselves. Such entry was always haunted by the spectre of women's initial entries into the academies as bodies not brains. Seen like this then, the spectre of violence against women as institutional culture is not the university's deviance, but in line with the very history of the university.

Even as substantial numbers of women now make up all levels of university communities, this institutional memory of their availability for use, probing, cutting, and disposal remains. Universities have not become institutions that seek to make women feel comfortable, but rather hanker after the golden age of the open objectification of women.

Saskia Goldschmidt surfaces the intersections between scientific pursuit, empire, gender, and sexuality in her novel *The*

*Hormone Factory.* In that book, contest over masculinity between two twin brothers, Mordechai (Motke) and Aron de Paauw, is also a contest over legitimacy. They tussle directly and indirectly over which forms of acquisitive, empire building – but also inquisitive, scientific masculine postures – are legitimate.

On the face of it, their factory is to make a women's contraceptive, which is very easy to see as a noble investment in the freeing of women to make choices over their bodies. However, Goldschmidt paints a universe in which women's bodies are valuable for exploitation as laboratories and labour.

This is as true of the women who work in this factory, enabling experimentation and wealth building by the brothers, as it is of the women who are chosen as wives and also exploited. All women are ultimately disposable in the terrain of medical science, and all women's bodies are cast as disposable.

The factory tests hormones on the women in Motke's immediate environment, but the tests are seldom consensual. When they appear so, the women characters do not know what it is they are consenting to. Motke's career and empire building seem premised on the well-being of women, but in actuality he demonstrates careless disregard for women's well-being. This is a paradox that is actually laid even more bare when we know that in Dutch 'hormone facktorie' means more than it does in English. Goldschmidt brought this to my attention at a shared panel at the Open Book Festival in Cape Town, outlining how the pun would be obvious to the Dutch reader. In the novel, she plays with this ambiguity too. Motke is a 'playboy' and a sexual predator.

In the schema of the novel, 'playboy' and 'sexual predator' are different on one level, even if they feed into each other. As a playboy, he is represented as engaging in consensual sex, even though 'playboy' status is not about polyamorous play, but about the trivialisation of women through anonymisation. The most famous playboy of the twentieth century, Hugh Hefner, who built a different empire and named it as such, understood this deception well. Taking advantage of the hard-won freedom language of feminist fights for sexual freedoms, he co-opted sexual rights for the oldest patriarchal con known to women: using women's bodies as currency for something that they could not benefit from, either individually or as a group. Hefner's was a spectacular con: eroticising the erasure of women, anonymising and animalising them. Eventually, they were no longer women, just 'bunnies' – interchangeable, consumable objects available to use against themselves. It is no wonder Hefner and Bill Cosby were such firm lifelong friends; they were both premier conmen, building careers on the veneer of advancing something liberatory, behind which hid their layered violence.

Hefner even called himself a feminist in the early days of *Playboy*, something two of my brilliant graduate students in media and gender at the University of the Witwatersrand, Dominique Rizos and Nwabisa Tsengiwe, never tired of being angered by. Motke is a character made in the image of Hefner and Cosby, or them in his, since the novel is set just before, during, and in the aftermath of the Second World War. Motke has the public face of an ally in women's reproductive freedoms, but he drugs women and manipulates their bodies, taking advantage of them in many ways. He reasons to himself that he walks a thin line between experimentation and sexual harassment. There is no thin line for Goldschmidt's reader, and there exists thin salvation for Motke, whose deathbed reflections and near remorse is the cause of these revelations that he built a highly successful pharmaceutical company on women's contraceptives, on women's pain, sexual abuse, and all manner of exploitation – from which he gained abundantly. Even this deathbed confession is not presented with clear remorse.

Motke's doublespeak is familiar to those of us who are attentive to women's histories across the globe, whether we have in mind the testing of Depo-Provera on Zimbabwean women in previous decades; the coerced and secret sterilisation of Aboriginal and Native American women; or the US's exported but now ubiquitous and glamorised pimp culture – systematic violence against women that relies on using women's bodies as exchange is a central part of empire building, and of science.

Sometimes science and empire-building work in obvious ways, and sometimes the relationships are less obvious. To trace them, we need not always follow the money per se, although this makes things easier. Sometimes, we have to follow the exchange. A Nigerian professor in the heartbreaking exposé that follows says, 'They pay with their bodies.' He understands this old regime well. That is how he is able to use language in this cruel and deceptive manner. The women are not involved in equal exchange, because they are 'pay[ing] with their bodies' for something that they should not have to pay for because they have already earned it.

This is one of the contexts against which I read the 2018 #SexforGrades and #SexforMarks scandal in Nigeria. The story I turn to now fills me with horrified rage. The only exceptional thing about it is the determined brilliance of the women who blew the lid wide open on it. The appropriate response to their work is not to celebrate them as heroic. It is to work with them, listen to every word they say, feel their fear, and make sure it stops.

In May 2018, Monica Osagie, a student at Obafemi Awolowo University (OAU) in Nigeria, had just finished editing a book for one of her male lecturers when suddenly, he asked her to sit on his lap. Upon refusing, he asked to date her, an invitation which she also rebuffed. The man was a professor and a pastor at a local church. He responded to her refusal with a threat to fail her as punishment. Soon thereafter, she failed a task for his course, and upon asking to see her script, since she knew she could not have failed, he refused, and reminded her, 'I gave you an opportunity and you missed it.' He then used hand signals to inform her that the solution to both the unseen script and the failure mark was to have sex with him five times.

Let me reiterate. She had met the academic requirement and was entitled to a mark; there is no academically defensible reason to refuse a student access to her own marked script. Any reason created – whether bureaucratic or predatory – is created for the sole reason of oppressive manipulation.

In various media interviews, she said that while this kind of abuse was commonplace – 'not just in Nigeria actually, it happens everywhere in the world' – most women students are afraid to report. The issue of reporting came up when she discussed what her professor had done to a friend of hers, immediately after the first event. As the friends discussed the event, Osagie realised that the burden of proof would lie with her. The professor had been arrogant because he knew he would get away with it, since chances of her reporting him, and of being believed, were slim.

It is important to note the multiple locations of fear in this scenario. Students are frightened to approach and be alone with their lecturers. They are terrorised when they rebuff the predatory advances of the same professors, and, as women raised in patriarchal cultures, and therefore fluent in the language of the Female Fear Factory, they know that shame will attach to their own violation and/or failure to complete their studies.

Just as she understands that women are afraid in patriarchal society generally, because of the Female Fear Factory, and specifically when they are being sexually harassed, Osagie knew she had to produce evidence that could be neither disputed nor dismissed. This is the burden of evidence that patriarchy places on those violated. This is how she was able to produce the audio recording of their next conversation, when she approached him for her script a second time. Arrogant in his power, he confidently repeated himself as she asked further questions, the answers to which left no room for ambiguity.

When Osagie publicly released this recording, the responses were unsurprising. Many students shared similar stories of experiences with the same professor, and with other academics – both at OAU and from other universities. Her strategic thinking eventually led to the dismissal of Prof Richard Akindele, who also later pleaded guilty to criminal charges and served a twenty-four-month sentence. He was convicted on four charges: two linked to soliciting and offering sex for marks, at twenty-four months each, and two for obstruction of justice, for twelve months each.

The judge ordered that all four be served concurrently. Although Osagie had successfully unmasked a sexual predator by producing the kind of evidence that is not always available, leading to a guilty plea and jail time for her assailant, and had met the unreasonable demands routinely placed on women who speak out against their sexual harassment, the university withheld her certificate. She still had no access to her script and was given two offers: either sit for evaluation again, or return to repeat the year. This is how universities respond to being challenged.

Even when they bureaucratically dissociate themselves from shameful, violent behaviour, they produce as little as possible by way of fully addressing the situation. Osagie's expectation that she should be given what is due to her if she has passed is not unreasonable. Nor is an expectation that there will be compensation to her, given the dangerous, violent setting that was created as part of her university experience. What is unreasonable and unethical is further aggression from a university that has already harmed her in such significant ways.

Osagie's actions may have inspired Kiki Mordi's undercover investigation into other predatory lecturers at the leading University of Lagos (UNILAG), or this could have been a coincidence. I read them as part of the same challenge to patriarchal violence, relying on similar gestures and logics, and with similar successes and costs.

In Mordi's short documentary podcast, 'Nigeria: Sex for Grades,' she reveals two more frightening examples of the sex for marks saga. Here, she goes undercover with another journalist known only as 'Kemi.' Mordi herself is a journalist and Lagos-based broadcaster who poses as a university student trying to gain access to a specific academic programme.

Structurally, the radio documentary has a narrator, identified at the beginning as Mordi herself, who occasionally makes way for the voices of other women students who have experienced sexual harassment by the subjects of her investigation. There is also a secondary narrator, Kemi, who takes up more space than the women offering snippets from their testimonies. As part of the exposé structure of the audio documentary, the senior academics investigated speak clearly in recordings that leave no room for interpretation of their intentions or thoughts.

Speaking to her motivation, Mordi reveals that she was sexually harassed by a lecturer in her student days in a phenomenon that has been part of the education landscape 'for decades.' Kemi shares this experience of also having been sexually harassed as a university student. Both journalists went to different universities, and so there is now testimony of this happening in at least four Nigerian universities. This evidence, alongside Osagie's and Mordi's statements, supports how widespread this harassment is. All the women are determined to prove what they claim. They are also all aware of how vulnerable other women on campus are.

This is what lies behind the oft-whispered advice to undergraduate women students not to go into the offices of lecturers alone. Here, as elsewhere, women are taught to avoid danger. And if they are unsuccessful in doing so, and then survive the violence, they are then pressured to produce evidence. Everyone may know the unspoken secret of how widespread sexual harassment of this sort is, but each victim or survivor will be isolated, treated as though they are presenting something unbelievable, and required to produce irrefutable proof.

Mordi notes early in the documentary that there are several names of predators from UNILAG that recur in the testimonies of women she has spoken to. The voice of the (former) women students, who ask to remain anonymous, speak of UNILAG lecturers whose behaviour includes 'groping,' 'locking office doors' to trap students inside, and 'dry humping' them. These voices draw on their own experiences, listing specific encounters which overlap but are not entirely uniform.

Kemi approaches Dr Boniface Igbeneghu, a senior lecturer and a pastor at Foursquare Gospel Church, whose name has come up several times in her investigations, and who is described as volatile by one of his former victims. While Mordi waits outside Igbeneghu's office as Kemi makes first contact, she is unceremoniously taken by the hand by another UNILAG academic, Dr Samuel Oladipo, whose name she recognises as that of the economics lecturer and as one of those that has also appeared in their research. She has had no previous encounters with this man, and he does not know her. However, not only does he touch her uninvited, but he also invites her to his office. Mordi then uses this as an opportunity to also pose as a student.

Inside his office, Mordi notes that Dr Oladipo is 'consistently inappropriate with [her],' referring to her beauty, calling her 'fine baby,' and leering at her breasts. Afterwards, he invites her to his office for private tutorials a total of three times, and eventually invites her to accompany him to the Senior Staff Club. The Senior Staff Club is a colonial hangover that is found in one version or another in many African universities. It is not always reserved for senior staff only; it may be open to postgraduate students, and, in some cases, may even be open to everybody who can afford to access it. In other words, different institutions have managed this legacy differently. The foundational logic of staff clubs was to ensure that there were spaces on university campuses where staff could both escape students and also be able to socialise with colleagues in an environment that did not transgress the boundaries of proper contact between students and staff.

In other words, the way in which these men use the Senior Staff Club – as is increasingly clear from what Mordi and Kemi uncover – is in direct contradistinction not only to the goal of ensuring hierarchical 'decorum' on one end of the spectrum, but also to the safeguarding of an ethical distance between students and academic staff.

In the meantime, Kemi is struck by similar patterns of behaviour. Both journalists give their age as seventeen, a year below the Nigerian legal age of consent, but old enough to be enrolled at a university. These young women work hard to make sure that what they uncover will not be watered down by the usual patriarchal covers used to defend violent men, such as presumed consent between adults. They provide their age as essentially children, minors – as defined by the Nigerian state. It is therefore impossible for them to consent, and these men know this, but because they are not confused about who has power here, age is irrelevant for the predators. Dr Boniface Igbeneghu comments on Kemi's beauty constantly, bizarrely asking of her that they pray. He closes his eyes as he says the prayer, and Kemi, keeping hers open, notices him 'jiggling his private parts' during the prayer. After the prayer, he questions her about her sex life.

When she questions the relevance of his questions, he insists that he is concerned as an older father figure. Kemi is not new to this strange, predatory behaviour:

> I recognise what Dr Boniface [Igbeneghu] is doing, I know what it feels like to be groomed by a university lecturer. I went to a different university, and it was nothing like I imagined. A lecturer began to target me. For two semesters, he withheld my exam results and pretended I never sat the papers. When I asked him to explain why, he repeatedly demanded to have sex with me. I never got a degree. I never graduated. The harassment forced me to drop out of university. I had nobody to turn to. No future. No money. It almost destroyed me.

This exploitative exchange has costs that go beyond the site of the violation itself. Kemi's realisation and analysis also link what Igbeneghu is doing to the systemic operation of sexual violence. It is a very clear expression of a deep grasp of how this particular system of violence works, and a powerful argument against individualising this experience as the odd behaviour of 'a few bad apples.' As a woman in a patriarchal world, fluent in the workings of the Female Fear Factory, Kemi knows that these links are important. This is grooming. It may not look exactly the same every single time, but it is a pattern of behaviour meant to prepare the student for violation by gradually wearing her down and priming her for ever-increasing violations.

Soon, Dr Boniface Igbeneghu too invites Kemi to accompany him to the Senior Staff Club, just as Dr Oladipo has done with Mordi. The club, as previously mentioned, is supposedly an exclusive space for senior university staff to socialise. However, both Mordi and Kemi know that several senior academics routinely invite young women to a 'Cold Room' in the club, a pattern of behaviour that is striking, as discussed earlier in this chapter.

When Kemi, feigning ignorance, asks how she, as a student, can be allowed in there, we hear Dr Igbeneghu's voice talking about how this is a room where they take 'girls' to 'smooch and romance.' He underlines that these women are taken there for 'benefits which are great.' Kemi wonders aloud about how this can be considered fair, but if Igbeneghu doubts his reasoning, it is not evident from his voice.

Pressing further, Kemi wonders aloud whether this is not also unfair to the young men undergraduates who have no access to this exchange economy. The associate professor of French sounds amused as he responds, 'It's not free for the girl; she's paying for it with her body,' at which point Kemi reminds the listener that this man is a pastor.

The contradictions here abound. As a pastor, he is one of the custodians of Christian morality, at the heart of which lie belief systems such as the sanctity of marriage as the appropriate place for any sexual activity, as well as a humane familial relationship between people that approximates Christ's unapologetic adherence to justice and re-humanisation. He knows this, as does she. This is why billions of people return to churches across the world, because these are spaces of salvation, recuperation, and community that are often so necessary in a world of deepening dehumanisation and isolation. But in another sense, churches are also just patriarchal institutions, with all the violence present in every other patriarchal institution.

This does not mean that Igbeneghu cannot be held responsible. What it does mean is that there are even fewer safe places for women. Kemi reminds the listener of the fact he is a pastor to link to something another witness says in the documentary, as well as to highlight how deliberate the extent of this man's predation is. These recordings of the predators saying unacceptable things leave them no room for ambiguity.

Kemi and Mordi also let other students speak under cover of anonymity if desired, while not standing apart from this experience, one which they are not just investigating as journalists, but in which they are also sharing. By placing their motivation up front, they are above question as they position themselves for a particular reading of the personal (as political). Survivors of sexual violence are often cast as speaking from an unjustified sense of vengeance when they take on men other than the specific ones who violated them.

They also speak to the institutionalisation of the phenomenon rather than it being limited to isolated cases, because they know that this is another form of dismissal that can be used against them. To use these senior men's own words in their own voices is brilliant, even if what they say is horrifying.

The mention of the Cold Room also speaks to the institutionalisation of this practice. It happens in a university space as a collective orgy of sexual exploitation, not in hidden, individual, unknowable spaces. Even those who attend the Senior Staff Club and abstain from this group sexual violence are implicated. The university is implicated, so it cannot legitimately claim ignorance. Consequently, the official response Mordi receives about a 'zero tolerance policy' to sexual harassment at UNILAG sounds hollow. The recordings of these identified men also throw down the gauntlet to UNILAG, rather than burdening students as usual to report and prove the existence of sexual harassment.

When Mordi eventually agrees to go to the Senior Staff Club, she is taken straight to what she recognises as the Cold Room from what the students in her previous investigations have told her. It is a space she describes as odd, with blackened windows and many young women being plied with alcohol and pressured to dance. She is constantly asked to dance by different men, asked to 'join them,' as they point to young women on the dance floor. When she informs Oladipo of her discomfort and starts to leave, he rushes after her and, battling to catch up to her on the stairs, reaches out and grabs one of her breasts from the back.

Mordi is already a survivor of sexual harassment, and this material is difficult to listen to. It is infinitely harder to have gone through it. However, because sexual violence is not considered violent, and evidence must be produced at any cost to stop violent men legally, these two women persist.

The voices of the previous victims of these men punctuate the journalists' narration of events, along with the important inclusion of the voices of these men. One woman insists about this humiliation, 'It's like a rite of passage. This is what female students have to go through.' As she says so, she is not addressing the two journalists, because she need not point this out to them. They are interviewing her for this programme, so they are gathering evidence of a process they know well. Secondly, they have both previously experienced sexual harassment by university lecturers at different universities. They do not need convincing.

Another victim was molested by Igbeneghu a total of ten times, including being groped by him while he wrote down scripture with his other hand. He sees no contradiction. The deception is so seamless he does not even try to mask it. It has been going on for several years, and she is not only no longer able to go to church, she has also tried to commit suicide four times. In addition to groping her, Igbeneghu told her that he would hand her over to another lecturer in his department and that, 'when he's done,' he would 'transfer [her] to someone else.' The victim adds, 'And there is nothing I can do about it because I won't graduate. I felt like I was better off dead.'

Here, again, the absolute crude clarity on the women as exchangeable, anonymised objects. For millions of people, church is a place of solace, but the contradictions are too high for the former student whose pastor-professor has robbed her of this space, of a place where she could have found renewal and healing.

Her isolation is complete as she is still unable to have any spaces of refuge, is unsure of herself, and is suicidal. All of this is difficult work: staying alive, going undercover, staying at university under these conditions. It is brutal.

Recognising all of this, these young women decide it must be exposed so it can be stopped. They are under so much pressure, in the very heart of the war against women, so that others do not have to go through the same ordeal. To ensure this, they gather evidence that may mean others like them do not have to.

Deciding that they need a little more information, but also nervous that the situation is escalating, Kemi accepts an invitation to Igbeneghu's office on a Saturday, where he immediately offers her non-alcoholic wine. She is triggered, but reminds herself that one of her colleagues is just outside the door, ready to burst in as soon as Kemi signals. These reminders are important, because this is a painful and frightening situation. She is still a woman, a survivor, alone in a room with a violent man.

Predictably, he asks her for a kiss and is angered when she says no. Here is that volatility one of the informants had spoken about. While trying to stay in character, Kemi reports that:

> My hands are shaking, my heart is beating, but I'm still trying to stay calm; I'm still trying to do my work as a journalist; it's one of the most difficult things that I've ever done in my life. After I refused to give him consent, he stood up and went to the bathroom for a moment. [Breathes deeply and whispers to herself, 'Stay calm, stay calm, stay calm.'] In my head I'm thinking, I'm this close to getting hard evidence on this man, so I had to weigh my options; to press the panic button or just wait to see how far he would go.

There is no gap between herself as journalist and as a woman; both those identities are here, like Lovera covering the killing of a woman very much like herself from a similar society, as examined in the chapter 'Femicidal Intimacy,' and Smith investigating a serial killer who was targeting women who may have been just like her in *Misogynies*. Kemi (and Lovera and Smith) is on the frontline, as is Mordi, and Osagie before her.

The fact that Mordi and Kemi are determined to unmask these violent and powerful men does not insulate them against the Female Fear Factory or the men's violence. On the contrary, it puts them on a collision course with them. But the hope that their work might create change for others is what motivates them.

Igbeneghu has once again locked the door. Kemi asks to use the bathroom, inside of which she speaks loudly to her colleague waiting outside about 'coming now.' The volume is for the benefit of the predator. It is not the sign for the colleague to burst in. As she comes out, he laughs at her and lets her go, but not before letting her know that there will be consequences if she does not see him again. He is arrogant. She is triggered.

Given how clear her fear and the enormity of the violence and damage is, to the journalists and their informant, his laughter is breathtaking. These women have paid dearly to gather this evidence. Asked for a response, UNILAG claims to be embarrassed by the behaviour of these two staff members, refers to its recent (2019) sexual harassment policy, suspends both men, and claims to be 'protective of student interest.'

Universities presented with this kind of information cannot just sit back and gloat that they teach students the exact ways to report violation. They have a responsibility to investigate the institutionalisation of predatory behaviour, not just case by case. It is bizarre that institutions filled to the brim by people highly skilled in getting information out of all kinds of contexts are found so wanting in gathering the required information to create safe spaces. Yet, when we recall that the sexualisation, sexual objectification, dehumanisation, and violation of women is part of the historic fabric of the university, a different picture emerges, one that is about the absence of political will to change, and one that is about refusing to recognise the full humanity and entitlements demanded by women.

Osagie and the two undercover journalists know that they are in danger if they take these men on, and there will be consequences. There is cause for fear. However, they understand that they are in danger anyway in patriarchy, as are other women. With that knowledge, they gather what they need to, to make sure these men can be stopped. They create a cost for the men, shaming them publicly, and equally importantly, they create a cost for the duplicitous universities.

Universities know this is going on. Women academics know, as do the male ones. Given the number of women in Nigeria saying how widespread it is, it cannot be a secret. How many women senior academics themselves underwent this rite of passage? We need to invest in ways that oblige universities to exercise a responsibility of care, not just pretend that these are isolated cases. We need to do more than just teach against violence, to actively create safe campuses. This is urgent. Policy is just one technical step. And I say this as a full professor who bears the scars of what it takes to have proper sexual harassment policies at one institution I previously worked at, the University of Fort Hare. I also bear the scars of the hostility that continued after its passing in an effort to actively undermine its efficacy. I also say so with extensive experience of what it means to be among a minority of senior staff who insisted that colleagues I worked closely with be held structurally accountable for what was revealed to be routine sexual harassment (and in the second case, serial rape) of women students at the University of the Witwatersrand.

These are not Nigerian universities. And I am pleased to say that at both of these institutions, feminist work continues to make sure that consequences are created and enforced constantly. But this is not work that universities can ever afford to be complacent about. It may not have been sex for marks at the institutions I mention above, but there is no 'better' sexual harassment and 'worse' sexual harassment. All forms of patriarchal violence ruins lives.

Speaking to journalist Tunde Fatunde, University of Benin's Associate Professor Ngozi Obiajulum Ilo says she is very hopeful that the outing of her predatory colleagues 'will serve as a deterrent to other ravenous wolves in sheep's clothing who call themselves higher education lecturers' – lecturers whom she herself also refers to as 'voracious lecturers.' I hope she is correct. However, I know it will take more than this. Women students and all students deserve so much more than predatory men being deterred or 'better protecting themselves,' which some will now learn to do.

Prof Elizabeth Katen from the University of Jos seems to think this the tip of the iceberg, asking 'Is it only sex for marks? What about sex for other things? What about sex for promotion?'

She, too, is correct, but the work will not do itself. Women professors may not necessarily be safe from violence, but they are institutionally more powerful than young women students. We may not need to go in with hidden recorders, but as expert knowledge producers, we have to come up with ways to gather the information and design the adaptive anti-violence measures that keep on working as we create safe campuses.

The messy terrain outlined above is very difficult reading. Sexual harassment at universities is often mired in so much nuance, double-talk, and technical red tape that it obscures how bloody it is. I have made a decision in this chapter to let three young women speak in their own voices, and to include, unedited, the additional words of the witnesses in Mordi and Kemi's exposé, because I remain unshaken in my knowledge that universities need to confront this work, not make it students' work or the burden of the – inevitably – minority of feminist academics who will engage in this work as one more aspect of the growing invisible additional labour we take on.

As Farah Deeba Chowdhury reminds us in 'Theorising Patriarchy,' sexual harassment produces constant insecurity as material effect and as affect, and fear of 'sexual harassment prevents women from participating in the paid labour force or politics.' We can add the academy to this list. She continues to outline the same in constructions of what she dubs 'public patriarchy,' which is about regulation of space and image: 'In the public arena women are only considered as sexual objects and patriarchy is maintained through sexual harassment.'

Yes, all universities need to do this work. All of them. Not only the Nigerian or South African or Indian or US American ones just because they have occasionally made global headlines.

# CHAPTER 8

# Foreign Familiars

'Intimacies generate complex pushes and pulls.'[74] – Phanuel Antwi *et al.*

The violent outbreaks of 2008 and 2015 across South African cities and towns mirrored each other: the vulnerable were 'foreign,' living and working in the margins amongst those who now disowned, hounded, and killed them. Victims were immigrants from African and/or South Asian countries. Helene Strauss's reminder that a third of the 2008 fatalities were South African citizens is a very important one.

In both 2008 and 2015, violence chose pathways of race, gender, class, and nationalist power in ways both obvious and blurred. The obvious ways lay in what was rendered visible in the media idiom and public talk: the race, class, and gender of the perpetrators posited against the origins and class of those attacked and/or displaced. On television and in print media, young Black men were shown as the perpetrators, going on rampages through economically marginal zones, although occasional images of women and children displaced were also briefly shown. The assailants were represented toyi-toying[75] and singing liberation struggle songs as they attacked, displaced, and killed those they had previously lived amongst. Obviously, this was about the intersections of nationalism, gender, race, and class, as all xenophobia is. The singing of anti-apartheid struggle songs as they killed people was highlighted as a particular irony and a source of much anger in the public discourse.

Public outrage assumed that the perpetrators were either ignorant of the past that had made the new South Africa possible, or just inexplicably monstrous. The violent outbreaks were met with mystification in 2008, and horror in 2015. President Jacob Zuma's 2015 assurances that such violence would never recur echoed President Thabo Mbeki's earlier insistence that the violence was mere criminality. Neither approach was particularly helpful; criminality and xenophobia are not mutually exclusive, while assurances of 'never again' ring hollow, since solutions can hardly be forthcoming for a poorly understood phenomenon.

From divergent quarters, the violators were deemed to be acting in contravention of African norms of ubuntu and the spirit of the Constitution, and as ignorant/ungrateful, given the continent's previous support for anti-apartheid liberation movements. In other words, the violators were in breach of the unwritten codes that make for proper new South African-ness. In the Filmmakers Against Racism's (FAR) film *Asikhulume*, musician Syd Kitchen is visibly upset as he declares, 'I am very ashamed to be South African today.'

How was it possible for these young men to be so unaware of the shameful contradictions they were performing? And how dare they sing struggle songs while killing Africans, when our immediate neighbours had paid such a high price to make sure that we had this freedom? Did they not understand that in the early days of their own freedom, ordinary Nigerians had paid a tax to subsidise exiled South African students? These sentiments were everywhere – written on the placards held by the tens of thousands who attended marches against xenophobia, espoused by those who offered media commentary and analysis, and felt by the ones who seethed privately. As they should have. But the attacks had equally vocal supporters. The vocal supporters are not the subject of this chapter, however, and there is much South African writing puzzling over these dimensions of the violence.

The victims took on tragic visibility. In 2008, the devastating imagery of the attacks was in the form of Mozambican Ernesto Alfabeto Nhamuave's body engulfed in flames. Adze Ugah's film *The Burning Man* follows Nhamuave's corpse home for burial, converses with a family in shock and devastation, and probes the contradictory relationship South Africa has always had with

Mozambican men's labour. In 2015, the assailants were once again young Black men from Alexandra township, not very different from those interviewed in Danny Turken's film *Affectionately Known as Alex*. The broken body on display belonged to another Mozambican man, Emmanuel Sithole, who was sometimes referred to as Josias by those who knew him alive. His was not a body on fire, but the end result was equally devastating: his skull cracked open.

Danai Mupotsa's work has taught us that boundaries of identity are policed and marked through rituals of production, even though they use a language of recovery. In these rituals of production 'coherent insides' and 'messy outsides' are cast as antagonistic. For the violent men in the streets and their supporters on the airwaves, the 'coherent insides' consisted of South African citizens, whereas the 'messy outsides' were occupied by selectively useful 'foreign nationals.' Most outraged South Africans, however, constructed the boundaries around (South) African legitimacy, amnesia, and being inhospitable.

It makes sense that the boundaries themselves were a site of production because, after Stuart Hall we know that 'as a process [identity] operates across difference, it entails discursive work, the binding and marking of symbolic boundaries,' so these boundaries are unstable. The production of 'foreign' is that of the conditionally undesirable. The production of foreigners is also the creation of vulnerability.

I analyse two short films, Xoliswa Sithole's *Martine and Thandeka* and Andy Spitz's *Angels on Our Shoulders*, to understand the connections between two forms of violent masculinity (heroic and aspirational) and Negrophobic violence.

The films were shot as part of Filmmakers Against Racism's (FAR) intervention during the 2008 outbreak. There is more to my selection of the two films I analyse here. Sithole's and Spitz's films refract the outbreaks through a language of the intimate and a focus on the everyday. These two very different short films reflect on nationalism, intimacy, masculinity, and the trauma induced by displacement through the lived experiences of women and girls.

Sithole's and Spitz's viewers are left to sit with what the experiences of these displaced women and girls illuminate about the gendering of xenophobic, Negrophobic violence, how it affects women, and equally, how it surfaces specific performances of masculinity. These films also manage to take seriously the horrific attacks and their traumatising effects on the interviewed women and children, whilst demonstrating the unspectacular nature of this violent masculinity.

Put differently, for Sithole and Spitz, as is the case for many feminist activists, creatives, and academics outside of the film industry, violent masculinities are both brutal and commonplace. The films invite us to think about the spectacle of the xenophobic violence as an expression of forms of masculinity that are threaded through what contemporary South Africa is. Sithole and Spitz make films that are profoundly and unapologetically about the lives of women and girls, and both filmmakers present us with women who retain interpretative authority. *Martine and Thandeka* and *Angels on Our Shoulders* are films about women, and they are also very sharp critiques of the brutality of heroic and aspirational nationalist scripts as violent. They are brilliant examples of an often-hidden dimension of how intimacy can be implicated in the production of female fear.

I have two intertwined arguments in this paper, and the films allow me to build these arguments in precise ways. My first argument is that gendered intimacy, rather than mere marginality, enabled the targeting of specific 'foreigners' for xenophobic attack. Many were taunted, physically attacked, and displaced by those they had previously lived with and amongst, not by strangers. In other words, in the violent outbreak, 'neighbour' was made into 'foreigner.' Class, race, and country of origin could also work as buffers against the construction of 'foreigner.' This was evident in who was safe against xenophobic attacks: those who hold passports from North America or Europe, those who lived in middle class and affluent areas, and those who were (sometimes) white. In the 2008 violence, the victims were African immigrants living amongst poor

Black people. In 2015, the displaced also included South Asians similarly resident. Those safe to brutalise were Black, (assumed) from third-world countries, residentially integrated into marginal Black South African communities.

In contexts of what Dorothy Driver calls 'intersecting marginalities,' intimacy is a double bind. While all human positions are intersectional, the phrase 'intersecting marginalities' applies to contexts where subjects are oppressed by more than one oppressive system. Driver's work exists in feminist scholarly tradition that has shown how the intimate space and relationship is a contradictory space of possible affirmation, recognition, and danger, as we begin to see clearly shown in Sithole's film, analysed below. In this chapter, intimacy is about the precarity of safety, and is haunted by risk/danger. In a previous chapter, 'Femicidal Intimacy,' I have expanded specifically on intimacy under conditions of hetero-patriarchal romance.

It is not always immediately clear, but the relationship of citizens to the state and the nation-state 'is constructed of intimacy' in multiple ways, as Irma du Plessis shows. In very different ways, Mupotsa, Antwi *et al*, and Du Plessis all agree that nationalist narrative relies on narratives of intimacy. For Antwi and colleagues, nationalist narratives additionally 'question the places and supposed non-places of intimacy.'

Elsewhere, Tyler and Gill remind us that gender-based violence and racism are also produced by/in contexts of intimacy. My second argument is that the perpetrators' choice of masculine performance rhymes with, rather than disrupts, celebrated post-apartheid masculinities. In one sense, both my arguments are about the manufacture of difference under conditions of sameness.

South African nationalism rests on heroic nationalism: the triumph of a just struggle over slavery, colonialism, and apartheid through the disavowal of fear. The courage and activism of the liberation movements are signalled as heroic masculinity in a multitude of ways: through the masculinist embodied spectacle, the foregrounding of men's activism, and the narrative of national founding fathers Mandela, Tambo, Tutu, and De Klerk.

Even the contestations of founding father narratives often posit a different set of inadequately recognised 'fathers of the nation': Sobukwe and Mandela. There is a vast archive of (southern) African feminist activist, creative, and scholarly critique of heroic masculinity which has painstakingly illuminated the dangers of heroic masculinity, including its erasure of women's activism and the normalisation of masculinist violence. I am thinking here, specifically, of different bodies of work, including but not limited to work of literary criticism on different South African epochs, including political (bio)graphy; women's activist (auto)biographies; feminist critiques of representation of women's activism in various genres; scholarship on women's movements and women's activist bodies; feminist activist campaigns and coalitions; writing on women and/at the TRC; feminist critiques of militarism; as well as criticisms of the accompanying tropes of the stoic mother/mother Africa and founding father.

Nonetheless, heroic nationalism continues to stand as potent shorthand for just political action in the social imaginary. Whereas heroic masculinity is the official foundational narrative and shorthand for righteous struggle, aspirational masculinity – often under the banner of aspirational nationalism – is the official nationalist transformation narrative. Put differently, heroic masculinity ensured that an old oppressive order was dismantled, while aspirational masculinity is about remaking the new nation. Neither heroic nationalism nor aspirational nationalism explicitly parade as masculinist. It has been the work of feminists and other gender-progressives to render the violently masculinist effects visible.

In aspirational nationalism, the first transformation is from poverty and disempowerment to a globally mobile, resource-acquiring, moneyed subject. The second transformation requires a specific orientation towards the world. The aspirational subject/proper South African is a financial explorer figure: the corporate man who sees Africa as an untapped market ready for his exploration, mining, and development. Aspirational nationalism celebrates the venturing of retail giants such as Mr Price, Spur, Steers, Nando's, MTN, and Woolworths into varied African markets. South African Airways branded itself as a 'gateway to Africa'; the South African-hosted FIFA World Cup tournament was called 'Africa's World Cup.' Brand South Africa invites pride, as does Proudly South Africa. Both are about selective exchange with the economically empowered of the world. In all of these exchanges, South Africa stands to benefit from 'going out' into the continent. However, the rest of the continent may not reciprocate. Aspirational nationalism's apex is unbridled capitalist masculinism.

South Africa's claimed economic development abrogates leadership to 'proper South Africans' (Mupotsa's 'coherent inside') while erasing existing economic cultures in different African countries (Mupotsa's 'messy outsides') to produce a 'lack' – a vacuum that can be filled with the goods, practices, and ideologies of an expanding project – that of the proper South African (wo) man.

## Martine and Thandeka

In Sithole's film, Thandeka, a Zimbabwean woman in a long-term relationship with a South African man, tries to make sense of both the outbreaks of violence and her partner's refusal to support her emotionally after her displacement with their children. She speaks lovingly of their romance and admits to the pain of his rejection when he repeats his desire for their children to leave the displacement camp so he can ensure their well-being.

In the film, she has moved out of their home, which is in an area where there have been attacks on 'foreigners,' but he stays. When they see each other – largely through her efforts, even though movement is easier for him as a South African man – he repeatedly speaks of how worried he is about his children being away from him, and not being able to see that they eat well. He longs for them.

Notably, he neither visits them nor expresses similar longing or concern for Thandeka.

Martine's story outlines layers of violations her family has undergone. She does not know the whereabouts of her husband and one child, without whom she had to flee the Democratic Republic of the Congo ('the DRC'). She speaks of the joyful surprise encounter she had with her sister, now working as a vendor on the streets of Johannesburg. She also experiences the terror of the May 2008 attacks and the secondary victimisation and threats of rape from some police officers entrusted with ensuring the safety of the displaced.

Both these women's narratives are the terrain of intimacy: romance, family, and sexual violation. At the same time, both show how the larger political processes express themselves through intimate violation: the instability of hetero-patriarchal romance, the ways in which political processes displace and separate families – first in the DRC and later in South Africa – and the violence of heroic masculinity across different localities.

Thandeka's narrative illustrates the workings of Driver's intersecting marginalities. As a poor, migrant Blackwoman, she has intersecting marginalities. She shares vulnerabilities with other women, and is left scarred by two expressions of masculinity: her partner's protective-father persona, which he expects her stoic compliance with, and the heroic masculinity of the perpetrators. The former shows the dangers of romantic intimacy for her as a Black, poor immigrant – after a lengthy relationship, she is disposable to her partner, can be rendered stranger/foreigner. Thus, intimacy as neighbour and as partner works as a double bind. In her narrative, she explains that her hurt comes from his recent inability to see her. His abandonment echoes her rendering as foreigner by the attacking men who knew her to be Zimbabwean.

Martine is also a prime example of the repeated rendering of neighbour as stranger. Ironically, South Africa prides itself on its exceptional status in relation to the continent. Yet, her life story shows how citizenship is precarious for women, regardless of whether one is in the country in which one should be able to exercise Antwi *et al*'s 'citizenship's rights,' or whether one is a refugee. Martine has suffered remarkably similar treatment in both the DRC and South Africa. In both, the state apparatus for her protection failed her. In Johannesburg, the police choose to secondarily victimise as well as directly threaten her with rape.

In both the DRC and South Africa, heroic masculinity does not serve the interests of women. Heroic masculinity is violent, and Martine has encountered it in two countries from groups of men ostensibly on opposing sides. There is remarkable synergy between the terrifying violence of the militarised Congolese men that lead to her displacement and the South African police who are supposed to protect her. The police are entrusted with these women's protection, but reinforce precarity instead.

For Sithole, here as elsewhere in her extensive, critically acclaimed oeuvre, women and girls' stories about their own lives are shaped by intersecting nationalism, race, patriarchy, and global capital flows. These narratives stand as more than first-person testimonies, as vital as these are, to speak about the violent project of nationalism across supposedly different contexts: one war torn and the other a stable democracy.

In her juxtaposition of experiences of politically motivated terror with the intrusion of the political into the familial across Zimbabwe, the DRC, and South Africa, Sithole's major characters, Martine and Thandeka – after whom she names her film – invite a reading of connections, as well as a questioning of the work that difference does. Martine and her family were comfortably middle class prior to the initial displacement, and it is partly their criticism of and activism against the Congolese government that put their lives in danger and saw them fleeing with nothing to South Africa. Her narrative amplifies the frailty of class in postcolonial contexts, as well the consistent gendering of large political processes.

Thandeka, too, offers significant insights about the frailty of post-independence democracy, hailing as she does from a country that once had the continent's highest literacy levels and economic stability, which saw it being dubbed 'the breadbasket of Africa.' In Sithole's films, these women, who speak with unapologetic pain and anger to offer sharp analysis of different nationalist, capitalist, and patriarchal processes, are the most eloquent illustration of how the personal is political. In these intertwining testimonies lies a cautionary tale about South African exceptionalism as we watch two articulate, multilingual women, one caught not just in nationalist violence but also in a familiarly confusing hetero-patriarchal matrix, and another whose previous life espouses the multilingual, well-heeled professional femininity South Africans conjure up through the trope of 'women's empowerment.'

Martine's previous life is the very embodiment of the 'proper South African woman' that aspirational nationalism seeks to achieve, as I have repeatedly written about elsewhere – and yet such status not only fails to protect her in the DRC, it also does not help her enter mainstream South African life, her fluency in the demands of 'proper South African-ness' notwithstanding.

Thandeka is very South African in a different sense. IsiNdebele, Thandeka's home language, is one of South Africa's official languages. To the ear, her fluency in isiZulu is that of many Johannesburgers. She is a woman of her city. Her accent in English is indistinguishable from that of many Nguni mother-tongue speakers.

The way that Zimbabwean Thandeka and Congolese Martine are cannot be lost on Sithole's viewers. It is neither their radical differences, nor a feeling of hostility towards a South African project or sensibility that one leaves the film with. It becomes clear that those who displaced them had specific knowledge about these women's citizenship. It is intimate knowledge that created risk and enabled both women to be re-made as 'foreigner' again and again.

## Angels on Our Shoulders

Andy Spitz names *Angels on Our Shoulders* after a line in Jeannette Sangi Thobela's story. Thobela's face and voice appear throughout the film. She anchors and frames, and her voice is often the defiant voice against the South African Department of Education's attempts to intervene in the crisis. In this film and others, Spitz returns to the intimate to highlight and critique forms of (non-)belonging. At the beginning of the film, Thobela speaks of several women with babies on their backs and shoulders, fleeing attacking men, heading towards the Primrose police station. Their safety, she suggests, is due to the fact that while carrying children, these women were protected by angels. She clarifies that although children themselves are angelic, additional supernatural beings ensured their safety.

Thobela's 'angels' explanation is how she grapples with the counter-intuitive attacks. Hetero-patriarchy romanticises motherhood, although it also routinely undervalues mothering, and brutalises mothers and children. The contradiction between the mythology of patriarchy about men as protectors of women and children (families) and the determination of the attacking groups of men is what Thobela grapples with. The attacks are also at odds with the script of good neighbourliness that intimacy promises. This produces not only trauma but also a crisis of meaning that is exacerbated by continued uncertainty because she continues to live under brutal conditions. The protection of angels is miraculous when the material world's resources are found wanting. It also posits the attacks as otherworldly. The only escape from what was previously unimaginable is recourse to the imagination, a retreat to fantasy and to faith.

This poignant narrative is haunted by the knowledge that others did not survive, something echoed by Benita Dumba and Fatima Nyamushwa, two girls interviewed in the film. Benita Dumba recalls how her mother pulled and carried her away in the nick of time, but how, as she turned back to grab her friend and playmate's hand, she saw the little girl collapse, wounded, onto the bodies of her slain parents. She repeats her longing for her friend – 'I need her' – underscoring how she tried hard to reach for her, to save her. The combination of what sounds like survivor's guilt, the trauma of witnessing such brutality by one so young, and attempts to understand why South Africans 'hate' those like her, is hard-hitting. Hate seems a fitting word here, not as a synonym for oppression, but as a means to explain how intimates/neighbours can turn against her family and others.

The film has no narrator, although text containing dates, geographical and statistical information appears, such as the deaths of sixty-two people and the displacement of two hundred thousand in the two weeks of violence in May 2008.

The film is shot entirely at the Rand Airport Displacement camp and begins with an unidentified, unseen choir singing the South African national anthem, a reminder of the brutality and paradoxes of nationalist zeal. Through the film, Spitz disrupts the mutating narrative of nationalism and provokes debate about its violence. She has screened the film at international film festivals and within South Africa, for the purposes it was shot, but also, significantly, at the camp in which she filmed.

The fleeing women, holding children, conjure up a familiar South African image: women with children strapped to their backs as they work and move around. The dangers of intimacy are further driven home when Thobela relates how school children had turned on those they taunted as 'Other' and foreign by chanting 'Mashangani, Mashangani,' an inclusion which brings intimacy, sameness, and the production of difference into collision.

As with Thandeka's isiNdebele in Sithole's film, XiTsonga – the speakers of which are sometimes (erroneously) called Mashangani – is one of the eleven official South African languages. Secondly, the children who have taken to taunting those made 'foreign' are their peers, another illustration of the dangers (rather than assurances) of intimacy.

In the 2008 and 2015 outbreaks, the locations of the xenophobic violence were as telling as spaces of safety. In both instances, location threw up for rethinking ideas about human worth, rights, and vulnerability. These xenophobic attacks may have defied 'commonsensical' ideas about sites of safety at home, in the street where one lives, among those one interacts with regularly, in stable democracies, among the known and trusted – they disrupted commonsensical ideas about neighbourliness and intimacy as sites of safety. Attention to extensive South African feminist analyses of the gendering of the transition from apartheid to democracy, the national narrative and memory process, the rape crisis, and so on, by known, and sometimes trusted, community members, should have disrupted these understandings of how violent power works in South Africa.

In other words, it may not be immediately apparent how the contours of this violence illustrate something about the Female Fear Factory. In fact, they rely on many of the logics of the Female Fear Factory.

First, feminists have long shown the ways in which home and intimacy can be sites of violence. This insistence has endured even as patriarchy has insisted on the fiction of the dangerous stranger, the monstrous violent criminal, and other forms of stranger danger. There are very clear connections between the explosion of violence in which neighbours and lovers turned on each other, and the structures of violence outlined in earlier chapters, 'Dangerous Fictions,' 'Mythologising Misogyny,' 'Femicidal Intimacy,' and in this chapter, 'Foreign Familiars.'

Second, the projection of monstrosity that we saw so excellently portrayed by Joan Smith in her discussion of the detective squad also finds echo here. In most media coverage, the xenophobic violence in South Africa is presented as mystifying, or as a result of poor people competing for resources. Perhaps it is these things.

However, it is a consequence of nationalism, and new South African nationalism in particular. The young violent men who are the face of xenophobic South Africa are performing with their bodies what South African business and the South African state routinely performs through money, visa requirements, and African campaigns. Rather than the opposite of affluent South African patriarchal masculinity, they are its enactment.

Post-apartheid South African corporate treats most Africans as useful economically but also disposable. The labour of migrants from southern Africa continues to be crucial for our mining economy. The language of neighbourliness as seen in 'African Renaissance,' 'African World Cup', and so forth are fleeting and opportunistic, whether issuing from the state or business. When we fail to understand the monstrous violent men, it is because of the blinkers we have on, very similar to the Ripper Squad detectives who failed to recognise the culprit was exactly like them.

Indeed, in the xenophobic outbreaks, we see the ways in which the Female Fear Factory can – and often does – travel on the back of capitalist logic. In Sithole's and Spitz's films, we see familiar patterns of violent masculinity at the heart of what is elsewhere framed as an exceptional set of circumstances. Sithole and Spitz point to the heart of this lie.

Together, *Martine and Thandeka* and *Angels on Our Shoulders* disrupt the narratives that suggest that anxiety about difference coupled with ignorance lies at the heart of recent xenophobic violence in South Africa. The violent xenophobes constructed as inexplicably monstrous are revealed to be very ordinary, and to also be the formerly intimate and neighbourly. The displaced and the victims were taunted, attacked, displaced, and killed by those who knew them and could identify them as 'foreign nationals.' Both films also debunk the narrative of the xenophobic violence as one that involved violent men attacking 'foreign men' by focusing predominantly on the experiences and interpretations of Gauteng-based displaced women and girls.

As Sithole and Spitz show, intersectional marginality produces instances where intimacy and neighbourliness present as sites of risk and danger, rather than one of unconditional security. Shared attributes between these particular victims and/or survivors and their perpetrators rendered them vulnerable to this kind of wounding.

Intimacy comes with dangers, especially for those whose identities are characterised by 'intersecting marginalities.' Gender power is experienced in those masculine and feminine expressions valued and aspirational, and, furthermore, in that these fêted gender performances are constitutive of citizenship, nation, and democracy.

Although the violent men on the streets were disowned in much public discourse as acting out of step with national norms, they were self-representing; firstly, in the idiom of heroic masculinity, toyi-toying in the streets, and secondly, performing aspirational masculinity in relating to 'Africa(ns)' as selectively and conditionally useful, and occasionally disposable. Both these are archetypical South African expressions of masculinity and maleness. When economically marginal men perform aspirational post-apartheid maleness, it is through their bodies and weapons. More powerful men have access to this physical, embodied power too. However, class advantage and/or capitalist power have other modes of enacting violence and fear.

Evoking a proud struggle lineage in the streets, these violent men marked the 'Others' as disposable, and themselves as engaged in a just, winnable struggle. This performance of public heroic masculinity in post-apartheid produces an 'Other' that is safe to violate through an inversion also seen during the Jacob Zuma rape trial. Once one side successfully performs heroic masculinity, triggering the required association with the anti-apartheid struggle, a specific enemy is created, one that takes on, symbolically, the characteristics of the historic enemies of that struggle, such as the apartheid state, the police, and the informers. The apartheid state and its police were powerful, and informants were dangerous. Consequently, all violence against them was self-defence, not just of individuals, but of the cause.

In the case of the xenophobic attacks, there was a cruel inversion, since those attacked were not powerful and/or dangerous and often shared the marginal status of their attackers, or occupied a more tenuous socio-economic position than their assailants.

The perpetrators were also performing aspirational masculinity, mirroring the symbolic violence that South African capital celebrates. South African businesses refer to 'African markets' available for mining and exploitation; 'African World Cup' for the 2010 FIFA Football World Cup, 2003 Cricket World Cup in 2003 and 1995 Rugby World Cup; and South African Airways as a 'gateway to Africa.' Afrophobic/Negrophobic South Africa sees itself in relation to the continent as exceptional, entitled, and superior, performing beyond the borders what these young men were already performing in their own communities. Both forms of violence are symbolic and material. Locked out of economic empowerment, the men on the streets use the resources at their disposal to enact with their bodies what corporate performs with capital. Unlike those with corporate power, they are unable to travel to an Africa that is 'out there' to inflict violence, recognising instead, all the time, that Africa is already here – in us.

It is also clear that 'foreigners' prone to physical attack are very specifically located within South Africa, and sometimes stereotyped as criminals and parasites. They are neither the wealthy, property-owning European and North American passport holders who settle in different parts of the country, nor the highly visible European criminals whose names have become household names, favouring the affluent suburb of Bedfordview in Johannesburg.

The attacks are never just about foreignness and crime, as the women in Andy Spitz's and Xoliswa Sithole's films clearly show. Twenty-two years after the country's first democratic elections, poor Black people are unable to fully access 'citizen's demands.' 'Foreigners' are prone to attack precisely because they are 'foreigners' from countries South African capital has marked safe to exploit, on the one hand, and because they attempt to integrate into everyday South African society, and live out neighbourliness and intimacy, on the other hand.

It seems like a paradox, but these 'foreigners' are open to brutalisation and looting precisely because their presence is simultaneously characterised by similarity to the marginal communities – whose lives are deeply inscribed by layers of violence – but also because of their differences from the communities. In this they are much like other groups in these communities that are prone to large-scale physical attacks, such as Black pensioners,

Black lesbian and queer youth – groups also characterised by intersectional marginalities.

In our understanding, it is clear that these attacks resemble, more than they differ from, the kinds of violence enacted on the bodies of those without direct access to power. It only appears paradoxical that violence takes on these forms when we ignore the insights feminist scholars (including a substantial body of writing within South Africa and other African academies) have produced about what kind of patriarchal violence is unleashed under any nationalism, and the risks of intimacy.

# CHAPTER 9

# Fearing Feminists

'For us women, the fight is daily.' – Marielle Franco

'The connections between and among women are the most feared, the most problematic, and the most potentially transforming force on the planet.' – Adrienne Rich

The late great Zimbabwean novelist and academic Yvonne Vera writes both hauntingly and beautifully of how bodies are trained over generations to enact patterns of fear and ownership. For Vera, the construction of collective fear is one of the ways in which the body and mind are disciplined, punished, and primed for oppressive control. In her novel, *Butterfly Burning*, she returns to these connections often. I will mention only two because these illustrate different aspects of the relations between fear and public space, connections which are also seen in the Female Fear Factory.

In writing a scene of the group-lynching of several men hung by their necks from trees in Rhodesia, she evokes a sight that brings back memories whilst pointing to what colonial masters achieved by leaving the bodies on display in this manner. Here, these bodies in plain view are an assault in many ways: to the humans thus treated, but also to the casual passer-by, the worker, the schoolgirl en route to school, the neighbour who may recognise a certain curve of the shoulder. In other words, the fear is in the details. The fear is also in the witnessing and the lesson that it could be you and yours.

To those who recognise one of the hanging men's bodies, the immediacy of the threat is communicated in the swiftness of a blink. To the passer-by, the knowledge of her own unsafety is introduced effectively, and so she begins to think (pointlessly) about how she might avoid being what Billie Holiday calls 'strange fruit,' because this language of fear, of race, of brutality as spectacle was well known in her part of the world too.

You are not safe. It could be you. Lesson learnt. Vera's second example is drawn from how she writes of Black bodies moving in Zimbabwean cities. Long after laws prohibiting natives from walking on the pavement, many of her characters move – defiant, lively, stylish, loudly through the city – but to a man/woman the body retains an inter-generational memory. Crowds manage this choreographed avoidance of the pavement and other similar spaces retained from a time – for some – before they were born, passed on unwillingly and unwittingly to them.

Thus, Vera teaches us that fear is not just present when we recognise it as such, a crucial reminder for the Female Fear Factory and its fluency. It is also sometimes present in cultures that resist the sources of the same fear. None of us are outside of the history and conditions of our unmaking. Whereas heroic masculinity posits that transcending or overcoming fear is the meaning of courage, and courage is the proper response to oppressive fear, I want to suggest that there are other interesting responses to fear. None of them are without consequence, but perhaps they teach us something, nonetheless.

I turn to the lives of feminists who are at once differently and similarly located, and their responses to the explicit exposure to amplified performances of the Female Fear Factory because they are feminists, and therefore position themselves in opposition to patriarchal containment.

When journalist Mona Eltahawy was arrested in Cairo, the police told her that they knew who she was. They were punishing her not just for the protest she was in the middle of, but for being herself, for other trouble she had made before.

They broke her arms in detention and sexually assaulted her. Because they did not fully know how to stop her, she found a way to borrow a phone in prison for enough seconds to be able to log into her Twitter account and announce that she had been arrested and state where she was. She does not say so, but she must have known that she could have disappeared without a trace, or been killed, or both. Like the women who send their jogging route or details of the taxi they enter to a beloved, she was making sure there was a place to start the search for her in the event of her demise. Women disappear. Activists are taken into police custody and disappear all over the world. It happens to activists of all kinds every day somewhere in the world. It also happens to ordinary people every day in some parts of the world.

The Egyptian police did not arrest only Eltahawy in Tahir Square. Many other women were beaten, broken, sexually assaulted in that movement by police and soldiers as well as by men who were supposed to be the women's comrades. There are no safe places for women; history has taught us that even radical political movements have rapists. It is important to remember that the Female Fear Factory claims space in revolutions. So much feminist labour has gone into teaching this lesson to us.

When Eltahawy sent that tweet, she was acting as badly as she had been by being part of that protest, building on a pattern of bad behaviour of whatever she had done to anger these police officers and to whip them into a frenzy to put her in her place, by showing her who really was in charge. Far from arguing that Eltahawy invited their brutality, she terrified them, and as prime agents of patriarchy, they reacted with extreme violence, as patriarchy always meets challenge.

Girls are taught never to make a man angry, as discussed in the second chapter of this book. Eltahawy refused this lesson, and claims 'anger' as one of the necessary sins in her latest book, *The Seven Necessary Sins for Women and Girls*. Anger is part of the arsenal we need to unlearn the fluencies of the Female Fear Factory. She tweeted and was eventually released.

Not long thereafter, Eltahawy managed to get herself arrested in her other country, the US. This time she was thrown into jail for spray-painting and defacing a subway poster in New York that was both racist and Islamophobic.

These are two events of institutionalised violence that were meant to teach her to behave, a lesson in compliance, in submitting to the Female Fear Factory. Both fear and violence are necessary for control. We are supposed to work ourselves to death avoiding fear and violence as women, even if it is futile, because we cannot avoid them, as I show in chapter 5 on the false promise of safety. Fear is exhausting. Exhausted women may not have enough energy left to revolt.

In her essay 'Terrified by the Voice of the People,' Isabella Matambanadzo teaches us that it is not only autocratic states that are 'terrified by the voice of the people,' but the systems they rely on to stay in power too. This is why patriarchy and white supremacy and all violent hierarchies use inversion.

Following Matambanadzo, then, if inversion cruelly marks that which violates us, then one of the ways we fight is by deliberately terrifying patriarchy. Feminists are already badly behaved women, but perhaps we need to be reminded of why. When feminist poet Shailja Patel named Tony Mochama as the man who had sexually assaulted her, and Prof Wambui Mwangi tweeted in support of her, they were both partaking in feminist praxis that many of us choose every day: supporting women who speak out against misogyny and violence against women. The ensuing furore dragged on for much longer than even the most serious contestations usually last on Twitter. It was not just a few days of shaming Patel and defending Mochama in ways that patriarchy's foot soldiers do. This event had many social-media afterlives, some of which arose months and even years after the original tweets.

Mochama's defenders kept them alive. Patel was cast as a mean-spirited, vengeful witch, and these accusations reappeared whenever she tweeted about gender-based violence anywhere. They sometimes reared their heads when she disagreed with someone on a totally unrelated matter. It was not just the usual folk either. Some of the attacks struck me as really about something apart from Patel and Mwangi's choices. It was also notable that even though several other women had tweeted support, some linking Patel's and Mwangi's to their own experiences with Mochama, the gist of the attacks on Patel was that she was unreliable, and had a particular axe to grind with Mochama and a few others. These accusations were not extended to Mwangi or the other accusers.

Then, Tony Mochama sued for defamation.

In 2020, a Nairobi court disregarded the statements submitted by Mwangi and Patel, the respondents in Mochama's lawsuit. The narratives contained in the statements were from women who testified that he had sexually violated them in various ways, as he had Mwangi and Patel. Mochama was awarded damages to the value of nine million Kenyan shillings and Mwangi and Patel were ordered to provide him with a public apology and retraction of their accusations. Nine million Kenyan shillings is a sizeable amount of money; in 2020, it could buy a small flat in the upscale suburb of Nairobi's Langata. In response to the court's ruling, Patel announced that she would leave Kenya, going into voluntary exile rather than ever apologise, retract what she had said and pay Mochama. This was a spectacular attempt to refuse to be held to ransom by a legal system that routinely says women's lives and their violation do not matter. The irony is that both Patel's and Mwangi's intellectual work amplifies strategies of undoing shame, hypervisibility, and insists on the necessity of continuing to craft new languages and modes of expanding freedom.

In her *Migritude,* Patel prompts us to reflect on ways of inhabiting the current African moment and indeed our own skins, standing at the meeting point of multiple inheritances of travel, displacement, hybridisation, and discovery in contexts of oppression and resistance. Mwangi's work is on how to think about economies of contestation across time. In her 'Silence Is a Woman,' she explores the (un)making of African independence and freedoms through projecting silence onto women. Both Patel's and Mwangi's works argue against the use and mythologisation of women's silence and oppression.

In the court case, many other women testified to being sexually harassed by the same man. In the public fracas, Mwangi was framed repeatedly as supporting her feminist sister and friend. However, she had testified to how he had also assaulted her previously.

The court documents are striking on several counts. The testimonies of women who name Mochama as their perpetrator are harrowing. Read against this litany, its emerging patterns, and guiding threads, the court's decision jars. At the same time, together, these documents point to the enduring power of the Female Fear Factory. They are also inspiring testimony to the determination of women who will not be crushed by that same fear and its threatening, institutionalised violence.

Faced with this verdict, Patel chose to leave Kenya rather than submit. Patel going into exile is a move that puts her outside of Mochama's jurisdiction. Patel's leaving the country also left Mwangi to continue to fight alone, to raise money and consider a long appeal process without the friend she had broken the silence alongside and in support of. There are many implications of this. None are simple.

How does a feminist make this determination?

It makes no sense to hold Patel responsible for any machinations of a patriarchal system which has the legal system at its disposal. This refusal to hold Patel responsible has to reside alongside the indignation we must feel over Mwangi's costly, administrative burden. Costly, administrative burdens are not clinical, unemotional affairs.

There is a cost to challenging patriarchy, and when taken to the courts, this is what it can look like. Like the Female Fear Factory elsewhere deployed, this process isolates and attempts to unmake relationships of affection and solidarity. Given the commonplace levels of violence meted out in daily life, it makes sense that the violence marshalled in defence of patriarchy is amplified in this manner.

It isolates. Patriarchal violence is isolating. It isolates through hypervisibility, as it has these two remarkable women. Their humiliation has to be staged publicly or it will not matter. This court case renders feminist dissent and solidarity illegitimate. Solidarity is a core feminist principle. We would do well to heed Sylvia Tamale's warning to brace ourselves to contend with 'a resurgence of cultural, economic and religious fundamentalist movements.'[76]

Each of the 'moments' I have alluded to, and spoken through, in this chapter, is illustrative of the emergent nexus of power and violence, fluent in established regimes while inaugurating new mutations whose traces are evident in locations beyond the studied examples. In another part of the African world, unknown assailants pumped four bullets into the bodies of Rio de Janeiro city councillor, Marielle Franco and Anderson Pedro Gomes, her driver.

Marielle Franco, a queer feminist and housing rights activist, was killed for being a woman and for being a woman in politics, according to Renatta Souza, who gives this insight in Juliana Ruhfus's documentary on Al Jazeera about the assassination of Franco. Souza, once Franco's chief of staff, is now one of the three Afro-Brazilian women elected to Rio de Janeiro's legislative assembly, alongside Dani Montero and Monica Francisco.

Franco's life was one of impossibilities, and her determination to fight against all aspects of the Brazilian superstructure meant that, although she was incredibly popular among the downtrodden from whom she came, and for whom she fought, she made many enemies. In a country where fifty-five percent of the population is Afro-Brazilian, and predominantly impoverished, Franco was one of two Black people at the prestigious Pontifical Catholic University of Rio de Janeiro (PUC) when she registered and subsequently graduated for her first degree, before going on to earn a sociology master's degree from Fluminense Federal University. She was also the only Black person on Rio's legislative assembly until her death.

Franco had spent most of her adult life engaged in feminist, anti-racist, queer, and pro-poor political movements. She had organised women in the favelas, worked tirelessly against the militarisation of policing, which always translated into first, further criminalising Black Brazilians for being poor and second, subjecting them to increasing levels of violence.

This was the ticket she stood on for one of the 51 legislature seats contested by 1,500 candidates. Her campaign slogan, 'Eu sou porque nos somos' can be translated into the definition of the philosophy of ubuntu (I am because we are).

After ten years at the Human Rights Committee, she had run for office in a country where most politicians are white men, standing on a ticket that stood for all the groups she belonged to that were routinely made invisible economically, politically, and socially in a country where collectively they – queer, opposed to police and military violence – were in the majority. A voice for single mothers, for people from the favelas, poor people, Black people. As councillor, she was also the chair of the Women's Defence Commission.

Shortly before she was assassinated with her driver, Anderson Pedro Gomes, on the evening of 14 March 2018, she had addressed a meeting of the Jovens Negras Movendo Estruturas (Young Black Women Moving Power Structures), where her last words were reportedly, 'We have to occupy every space with our bodies.'

Rage and grief exploded in the aftermath of her assassination in Rio and in marches across the world. The movements she belonged to, and the people she fought alongside and on behalf of, ensured that three women were voted into the structure in which she had previously been alone. Three years later, there is now a mass movement that continues to keep her memory alive, to demand that those responsible for her murder be brought to book and a clear explanation for her killing be provided. While two former members of the police force would be charged for her murder, there remain many unanswered questions about their motives.

The pressure also comes from the international community, whose support and grief surprised even her fiancée, and occasional partner of thirteen years, Monica Benicio.

However, the aftermath of her death has not always been a deepening of the politics she stood for and fought so hard for. Ironically, her assassination and the subsequent investigation was used as justification for further militarisation of the favelas. But the movement for change, which is also a movement that always resists the brutality of this very militarisation and its ties to state corruption, shows no signs of slowing down.

As Benicio said when asked on the BBC Outlook Programme, while 'what happened to her was barbaric,' Franco's legacy is that of a fight against machismo in favour of the lesson that politics can be carried with affection.

Even alone, or one of two in different spaces, Franco defied the odds, and as she angrily shouted back to hecklers when she was on the podium, she refused to be silenced by anyone, especially those who did not 'know how to listen to an elected woman.' Her assassination was an attempt to silence and interrupt her.

The tens of thousands who still come out into the streets, in concerts, marches, and even in carnival – with her name and face displayed, into streets that bear her name – continue to keep her alive. As campaigns, and on t-shirts, banners, and graffiti, 'Marielle Vive,' which means both 'long live Marielle' and 'Marielle lives,' is a direct refusal to accept that they could silence her. And it seems, as frightening as her vision was for the Brazilian elite, her assassination has simply amplified it. They may have killed her body, but the people she showed up for continue to show up for her.

It has become commonplace for marchers to not only respond 'Presente' in response to 'Marielle,' but on marches linked to any – or all – of the causes she cared about, banners, t-shirts, bags, placards, flags, and pins declare 'Marielle presente' and 'Anderson presente.'

Although patriarchy uses violence to enforce fear, and to punish those who will not successfully be made female, and submissive, it cannot kill feminism. Although agents of patriarchy and the state – through the courts and police force – may attempt to silence and bankrupt and kill those who rise against it, hundreds of thousands more will sprout and amplify the project of disrupting patriarchy, interrupting the Female Fear Factory, and unlearning its fluencies everywhere.

# CHAPTER 10

# Safety, Nationalism, and COVID

'I am learning to live beyond fear by living through it, and in the process learning to turn fury at my own limitations into some more creative energy.'[77] – Audre Lorde

'Shame is a part of conflict, and current global conflicts have reinserted a sense of shame onto the public stage. However powerfully shame is recognised and represented, it has neither a single face nor a common language. It exists rather in fragments – in cultural detritus left over from unexpected trauma, and in the imagined spectres of fear, loathing, loss and fright.'[78] – Penny Siopis

In her *The Cancer Journals,* Audre Lorde writes of the necessity of thinking about the ways in which illness, medical science, patriarchal societal expectations, and the capitalist interests of pharmaceutical and other industries intersect. The disease is both a physical and deeply emotional experience, and neither of these exist outside of the political definitions that accompany her embodiment as a Black lesbian woman. Lorde's battle is to find a language in which to speak about the cancer, the pain, the isolation, and the shame as political.

She was writing of her experience of cancer, and the battle to make freeing decisions whilst under the deluge of medical advice premised on ideas about her body and self she dare not capitulate to. When the pandemic first started, whereas much of the analyses of the virus focused on the medical, and viral mapping and immunologist dimensions, it soon became evident that COVID-19's full impact could not be fully grasped through exclusive attention to the medical and hard sciences, important though these inquiries were.

As the pandemic held the world in its grip, it became clear that while the scale of its reach is unprecedented, socially, economically, and politically, the pandemic mapped itself onto pre-existing patterns. It also held lessons about those who would be deemed 'essential,' and who among those would be celebrated and/or made invisible.

Whether countries decided on hard or soft lockdowns, or eschewed lockdowns altogether, there was consistent emphasis on safety. Here, safety was mentioned explicitly in relation to safety from the virus, through following the advice of the World Health Organization, medical doctors, and other scientists. And so it is that the world took to wearing masks en masse for the first time in a century, but on a decidedly larger scale than was the case during the Spanish Flu pandemic.

In many lockdowns, since the source of danger was any body, and anybody, emphasis was placed on disciplining the body through hygiene and isolation. Hygiene involved the wearing of masks to avoid infecting each other through droplets from breath and saliva, as well as obsessive handwashing and sanitisation. Isolation included calls to stay home and maintain physical distance, and talk of 'new normal' ways emerged, of working or schooling alone, by communicating digitally. It also entailed a retreat to thinking about ourselves as countries again, and nationalism reared its head in many unpredictable, albeit not new, ways.

## Staying at Home

Staying at home was repeatedly framed as the responsible thing to do, to ensure decreasing infections, unless you were one of those deemed 'essential workers.' Essential workers occupy a long continuum of people from the visibly celebrated medical doctors, nurses, and other health workers to journalists tasked with keeping the world abreast of developments, to the taken-for-granted service workers in our supermarkets, pharmacies, and petrol stations. Even more invisible were the workers whose labour ensured that the supermarket shelves were stocked, unable to stay at home because animals needed to be slaughtered, bread needed to be baked, and vegetables and fruits needed to be picked and packaged, stored, catalogued, and packed into trucks driven by equally unacknowledged drivers moving across large distances and multiple borders.

But if staying at home was the minimum requirement to ensure safety, this was not always an option. In what follows, I highlight the inadequacy and pitfalls of national and multinational safety calls by reading the responses by writers and activists who refuse the call to compliantly stay at home, disbelieving the promise of safety, and making urgent calls for a remade world, not one whose oppressive structure is given free rein to crystallise under the banner of fear. I read these texts alongside (and through) the works of two artists – Lorde and Siopis – produced long before the COVID-19 pandemic began. Although the pandemic continues to terrify most of the globe as I write this chapter, countries in the global North have rolled out vaccines, while preventing the equal sharing, manufacture, and circulation of the same to the global South countries. The full story of the pandemic is yet to be told, as, indeed, it is impossible to fully grasp the scale of the impact without the benefit of hindsight.

This is not to say that there have been no areas of illumination. Far from it. Writing in the first few months of the pandemic, Sisonke Msimang agonises about the emerging meanings of home. Raised in exile in various East African countries and Canada, and now resident in Australia, with most of her birth family back in South Africa, Msimang insists on complicating the taken-for-granted status of home as safe, available, and stable. In her essay 'Homesick: Notes on Lockdown,'[79] she points to the various problematic dimensions that accompany invitations to stay at home as an easy way to access safety.

Msimang has three main problems which lead her further away from the blissful self-isolation of meditation apps she sees all around her. Instead, she worries on the page, and feels a creeping sense of grief. First, Msimang knows that safety is a double-edged sword for women. It is often 'the loss of what little freedom we have,' and it is precarity when they 'live in homes where the air is thick with tension, where a "wrong" move results in days of pain, this time will be interminable.'[80]

In many parts of the world, the freedom to move in and out of the home is one that was hard fought for. It is still not guaranteed to all. Home is also embattled terrain for many women, where there is tension and/or violence in the home. For these categories of women, the pressure to stay at home comes not with the assurances of safety, but with the fear of confinement and violation by others within the home.

In another part of the world, staying at home renders women unsafe from police violence, not the violence of those they share a home with. For two African-American women, Breonna Taylor – shot while sleeping in her bed – and Alteria Woods – shot inside her boyfriend's home, both killed by police officers who were later exonerated, there is no safety at home. Twenty-six-year-old Taylor and twenty-one-year-old Woods were shot within days of each other in March 2020 in Kentucky and Florida respectively, in the United States. These two women join a long line of Blackwomen killed with no consequences by US police officers from whom they cannot expect safety and protection.

Notwithstanding the talk of medical leaders and politicians, safety is never a neutral category. Instead, it is shaped by other axes of power which may increase or minimise vulnerability to private and public violence. Msimang's refusal to accept a straightforward connection between home and safety is informed by the knowledge that the safety of home is shaped in ways that can be deadly depending on the race, gender, sexual orientation, class, and the proximity to power of those at home.

Second, she worries about 'what it will mean to be in the house together all the time with those you love, or no longer love, or wish to love more.' While it is possible to imagine an idyllic situation with beloveds in a comfortable home setting, domestic and family arrangements often provide other challenges. Here, she points to the emotional labour entailed in heightened proximity; but by implication, there are additional forms of labour when there are multiple occupants in the home.

Msimang's concerns here intersect with those of another feminist writer, Kharnita Mohamed, who highlights the problems with the movement into the home framed as safety above all things. In her 'Remaking the Ordinary,' Mohamed reflects on how working from home brought unrealistic expectations from employers thus:

> [A]cademic staff were imagined to be superhumans, immune from illness, teachers could magically whip up online curricula and run households with homeschooled kids and ageing parents, plus care for friends and lovers and siblings, while frantically sanitising the groceries they brought into their homes.[81]

The picture that emerges from reading Mohamed and Msimang is that home is far from the safe environ proposed by the medical and political leaders tasked with finding solutions to the pandemic. Mohamed argues further for the reconsideration of all 'normals' to create equitable worlds that learn from crises. In this urgently needed normal proposed by Mohamed, all men 'know how to care and nurture, so that women and children can go wherever they please, and relax in their homes, unencumbered by fear and predation.'[82]

In paintings from her 2002-2005 *Shame* series where she offers several human forms accompanied by repeated stamp patterns, Penny Siopis visually revisits the ideas about home that continue to circulate in the public domain, feminist problematisation notwithstanding. The images in this series use her signature pinks, reds, oranges, and browns against a white background.

All the paintings resist easy consumption or interpretation: the figures and the words stamped on each page complicate the painted images. The individual images are shown together in exhibitions and are not individually named.

While there are several themes in this series that lend themselves to thinking about the complications of home, family, safety, and confinement, I focus on a few on which the words 'Home is where your mother is' are stamped. Importantly, the juxtaposition of the text of the stamp with the disturbing images invite readings of childhood, and specifically girlhood, in increasingly complicated ways. The disjuncture between what the stamp suggests and the pain or vulnerability of the painted image invites us to pause.

If the stamp's lettering suggests easy comfort and happiness, it is directly challenged by the images, many of which are not easy to decipher. In this exploration of 'the poetics of vulnerability,' Siopis juxtaposes cheerful-sounding stamps with disturbing painted scenes of contorting bodies, lines that suggest cutting and bleeding on the page. This suggestion of bleeding and leaking bodies is further strengthened by the artist's chosen colour palettes.

'Home is where the heart is' is stamped on fifteen disturbing images that portray contorted figures, girls and other childlike figures in various trapped, pained positions, sometimes with adult hands covering their mouths. In one, a dark, childlike, blindfolded figure on all fours is set against a white background with red streaks. The same stamp pattern appears on a different image with a large, dark, crying face, and yet another presents an inverted, foetus-like figure with her stomach cut out. In a third and fourth, girl figures are trapped. The third wears a red dress with a white collar; she is trapped in a barbed wire vortex, with hands raised in self-defence. The final one is shown in profile. A girl kneels, her wrists in chains. In the distant background, we notice that the chain leads to the neck of a white, floating figure.

The foetus-like image presents the profile of a floating figure with her stomach hollowed out so that the insides are visible. Both the figure and the stamp occupy the left side of the frame, the figure's legs bend at the knee out of the frame. The figure appears mobile, about to float out of the frame immediately after the stamped arc. It is a haunting figure, and the mixture of oil, lacquer, and enamel paints with glue offers a nearly transparent view of the abdomen and enhances the sense of the image as a mobile one.

True to the image's textured and mobile qualities, the meanings suggested by the painting proliferate. It could be a pregnant body, even if the foetus also resembles a wound. The figure's skin moves from a deep red face to barely pink feet. It is as open to joyful reading as it is to troubling. It is a tension the painting invites as the painter refuses to provide us with clarity.

In another painting, a large, deep-red, crying face dominates the frame. 'Home is where your mom is' is stamped once, neatly in the top right corner. In a third still, a supine body, dressed in pink, save for ballet shoes, drips with what approximates blood. The figure lies horizontally across the frame, in the bottom half of the page. The stamp forms an arc over the head and leaks off both the bottom and top of the page.

The latter two images are unsettling, made more so by the stamp. We do well to remember that they form part of the artist's *Shame* series. Siopis has described lacquer paint as sticky and hard to work with, yet its interactions with her other paint offer unpredictability, and productive uncertainty.

In these particular images, shame is explored in relation to submission and play in the figure on all fours; pain and shame in the crying-face image; whereas the sites of reproduction and modes of mothering are themselves called into question in the inverted foetus figure. The final figure echoes slavery, in posture and artistic rendering, which echoes abolitionist pamphlets.

All the paintings are mnemonic engagements with the idea of home, and shame's intrusions into that space. In her catalogue essay to *Shame*, Siopis links these images to both a language of capturing and referencing trauma and writes, 'I thought how so much childhood hurt, real or imagined, grows with us, over and over again, as shame.' These images carry traces of violation and hurt. Their rendering, however, works to evoke empathy in the viewer once the struggle for absolute clarity of what lies within the frame is surrendered.

It is this preoccupation with things that do not easily go together that both troubles and enchants in Siopis's visual theorisation of subjectivity, home, and shame. In this series, shame is everywhere in the home – in the stamps repeating apologies, clichés, mantras on love, as well as Hallmark holidays.

In the home, safety is slippery. Not all the images of hurt suggest victimisation. Some appear to be accidental. Yet, hurt is everywhere. Siopis, Mohamed, and Msimang offer divergent, generative languages with which we can think against multinational, patriarchal erasure when home is reinstated as an unproblematic zone of safety.

Thirdly, Msimang writes, 'I live in Australia but almost everyone I love is in South Africa, and so I am homesick, prevented from coming home by a web of travel bans and health warnings.'[83]

The irony outlined by Msimang is an important one. For many migrants, who make up a sizeable percentage of the world's population, home is far away. Lockdowns also saw us retreat into nation, and sometimes nationalism, as borders closed for national security. In a world increasingly imaged as a globalising one and in which the borders are said to be permeable, lockdowns legitimised this retreat to the grammar of the national. We would do well to remember, as Frassinelli writes, that '[b]orders do not simply divide the world. They configure it. They impede and at the same time channel a multiplicity of fluxes and movements.'[84]

Far from being inconsequential, this retreat will have far-reaching effects. For women, the gender for whom nationalism seldom works, the reconfigurations matter. There is another meaning to home that defies this national sense of boundedness, as Msimang reminds us. For her, home is mobile, not just because of the exile experience, but more so because of the widely shared experience of migration that renders multiple homes possible. Therefore, the invitation to 'stay home' is untenable, because she is at home and unable to get home at the same time. As she explained about her essay in a conversation with me and Melinda Ferguson, publisher of *The Lockdown Collection*, part of what has made being away from her South African home post-apartheid possible, once her family could return freely, was the knowledge that she could always return.

The COVID-19 configuration of space has complicated what is possible. Approaching the relationship between travel, nation, and COVID-19 from a different angle, Everjoice Win looks back at the HIV/AIDS pandemic, notices connections between stigma and travel in emerging Zimbabwean attitudes to COVID-19 in its early days, and worries anew. She writes:

> COVID-19 is now here with us. There are many lessons we learnt from HIV & AIDS, the most important one for me is that denial, stigma and discrimination kill the soul, more than a virus destroys our physical bodies.

It is the associations between travel and the new virus that raised Win's suspicions, especially when the Zimbabwean public mood shifted from worrying about European tourists at the beginning of March 2020, to treating Zimbabweans returning home from neighbouring countries with suspicion.

It is important to be mindful of history. Win reminds us of how costly the HIV/AIDS stigma was at one time.

## Safety and Protest

As lockdowns tightened across the globe, news filtered in of forms of abusive policing and excessive violence used against marginal subjects in many cities across the world. As devastating as this is, it should be unsurprising, because in order to convincingly maintain the calls for safety, the presence of fear needed to be highlighted. For some countries, the pandemic's mere presence was not enough because fear needs symbolic violence.

However, for those already systematically rendered precarious and therefore violated with impunity, a virus did not dampen the urgency of protest. Indeed, despite lockdowns and the exceptional national consciousness they sought to inculcate, policing in South Africa, Kenya, and Nigeria showed that police officers do not execute their duty to serve and protect indiscriminately. Perhaps, they imagined their reign of terror unquestionable.

In Kenyan cities, at the end of March 2020, police enforced lockdowns and COVID-19 mandated curfews by unleashing violence on citizens so severe it led to country-wide protests. In what started as an overzealous and brutal attack on commuters using ferries in Mombasa, riot police threw tear gas and bore down on unsuspecting citizens, forcing some to lie down on the ground. In Nairobi, thirteen-year-old Yassin Moyo was shot and killed by the police while standing on a balcony with his siblings.

These were two of many similar instances of police brutality unleashed on civilians. This brutality was met with widespread demonstrations across the country, condemnation by human rights bodies, and ongoing lawsuits by different Kenyan families and activists.

In South Africa, it was the similar disregard for ordinary, and especially marginalized, people that saw the South African Police Service and National Defence members assault Collins Khoza in his Alexandra township home for drinking alcohol in his yard.

However, as multitudes took to the streets for Black Lives Matter solidarity marches across the globe, we saw equal energies in feminist organised marches in Nigeria and Namibia to shut down those countries, holding governments accountable for their brutality against citizens in physical and symbolic ways.

In Nigeria, the Lekki massacre was the devastating result of a sustained, nationwide series of marches spread out over several days. For several days, activists in Namibia also stayed out in the streets as part of the #ShutdownNamibia protests for responsive action against gender-based violence.

Their states may have been circulating 'safety' and national interest, but the Namibian and Nigerian feminists knew that nationalism was a con. They understood that calls for national consciousness and safety sacrifice women's well-being, and feed on our blood. They also understood, as Phadke reminds us, that '[s] afety that is linked to surveillance or protectionism can only be understood through sexist and paternalistic logic,'[85] and that the safety being produced was not theirs. In choosing risk, therefore, they asserted that 'what women need in order to maximise their claim to public space as citizens is not greater surveillance or protectionism (however well-meaning), but the right to engage risk.'[86]

Finally, as these activists took to the streets, they revealed the lie in the promises of their respective states, revealing the many ways in which – as those who always fell outside of the definition of who could be rendered safe – their demands were urgent.

To take to the streets in record-breaking numbers during a pandemic is not recklessness. It is clarity on the use of fear for control, as well as the importance of asserting the right to recognition even during a pandemic.

In other words, when Blacks in the US fall outside of who the state chooses to render safe from the pandemic, or women and queer folk take to Namibian and Nigerian streets because 'safety' and 'nationalism' are once again used against them, this is a radical call. It is a refusal of the slippery talk of safety and an urgent claim to full recognition.

The political uses of fear do not pause under a pandemic. The Female Fear Factory continues unabated and needs interruption just as vigorously as ever during COVID-19, where fear and crises are sometimes heightened as an excuse to plunder. While a real virus rages on, we have seen widespread corruption, violence, and greed continue. These activists understand that their work in dismantling the systems that thrive on manufacturing fear cannot abate.

# DEPARTURES:
# Refusing the Prison of Fear – A Diary

*Eastern Cape, 1972-1980s – December*

During summer holidays, we sometimes spend a week or so at my Nkgono's home in Motlokofane, Matatiele, my maternal ancestral home to which my grandparents returned on retirement from their Johannesburg life, long before I was born.

These visits to Matatiele are fascinating excursions that I do not enjoy as much as I am fascinated by how different life is here from our regular life in our small university home town of Alice. There is no electricity here, so to me that means everything must be harder. But the adults still manage to make everything happen. It is impossible to keep track of the specific ways I am related to all the members of my enormous extended family who live here. I take cues from the specific way they address me. I love being addressed as Mamane (maternal aunt), Rakgadi (paternal aunt), and Ausi (sister) here. An aunt and a big sister are wonderful things. The titles sound silly in English. I come from people who use 'cousin sister' when speaking English to build a bridge between two incompatible ways of understanding family.

'Cousin' suggests extended family, 'cousin sister' is a refusal to see her as anything but another sister, and therefore immediate family. And so I am 'aunt' to all my cousin's children exactly as I am to my sibling's offspring.

But it can be tricky deciphering what to call the ones who call me Dineo or Pumula. My sister Lebo knows exactly who everyone is here, but she isn't always able to tell me. The ones I don't remember always ask me if I know who they are. And I decide to lie to avoid offending them. My version of the lie is simple. I feign offence at the suggestion that I could ever forget them, since I am obviously related to them.

There is another lie that we go along with. I let them unnecessarily mangle my Xhosa name, wondering why they cannot just use the Sotho one. There is a lot of on-the-mouth-kiss greeting, the thing I like least about being from the Eastern Cape.

Because Matatiele is rural, my sisters and I roam over what seem like endless landscapes – to a family member's house a kilometre away in one direction, a stream in a second direction, and in another, my grandmother's plot, green with plants I do not immediately recognise.

My second favourite thing about Matatiele is how my mother's brothers sometimes let me ride on their horses with them, even though girls and women do not ride horses here. It is a taboo, but they give in to my pleas until I turn self-conscious and stop asking, the year I turn 11.

The absolute best thing about Matatiele is anything to do with Ntatemoholo Mabusetsa. Although he is technically my late grandfather's half-brother, as far as I am concerned, he is all the grandfather I need. He is the only one I get. I find him infinitely fascinating, and there are no limits to his indulgence of me.

Everybody in the family is baffled. He is notoriously prickly, but not with me.

The arrival of puberty comes with a new warning on our trips to Matatiele. I know I see fear flash briefly across her face when my mother explains that adolescent girls are sometimes abducted by strange men who plan to force them into wifehood. But I am a child, I protest. Afterwards, as we wander off, my cousin Senate confides in me that these men from distant villages who still practise this custom consider girls who wear trousers immodest and inappropriate wife material. I wear nothing but jeans and shorts for future trips no matter what the temperature is. She continues wearing dresses. She is not afraid. My father and uncles will kill them, she says. Her father is my mother's elder brother, so her uncles are mine too. But how would they find us? And how long would it take? We don't say 'the rape,' but we fear this is part of this abduction business. Senate, like my sister Lebo, can be very strange. They get scared of the wrong things. I keep on wearing shorts, and I stoke the flames of my red-hot rage against a world that sees wives in children.

### *Inanda Seminary, Natal, 1985-1987*

Imagine my shock when I arrive at my boarding school outside Durban and hear about another version of the organised kidnapping of girls by men. This time, it is not mysterious village men who lay claim to an old tradition for legitimacy.

This new thing called 'jackrolling' leaves me cold. It is narrated by the lips of schoolmates whose homes are in the Transvaal townships. Soon enough, peers from Cape Town tell a similar story about abductions by gangs called 'iintsara.' Jackrollers and iintsara are township gang rapists who may dabble in other crimes too. Some of them are teenage boys.

I know that the world is unfair to girls, but this is strange. Groups of young men, who have nothing in common, are abducting and gang-raping Blackgirls in rural and township South Africa. I do not understand this. As if there aren't enough things to worry about with the unpredictable, menacing white soldiers in townships or apartheid policemen of any race.

### *Cape Town, 1995*

I read a newspaper report of a man who broke into a sleeping woman's flat in Gardens. She lives on the third floor of a building, but he manages to climb through her window. When she comes to, he is on top of her. I remember no further details about the story. I can think of nothing worse, even though reports of rape have been commonplace for as long as I have been aware of rape as something that exists in the world.

I am a very busy young woman. I am a graduate student at the University of Cape Town, a tutor in two different departments at this university, and a tutor at the Cape Technikon. My boyfriend and I go clubbing to the same joint with a group of friends every Friday and Saturday night. They play a lot of hip-hop and R&B, and we are all obsessed with the kwaito group Boom Shaka. Yet, with all of this going on, I still have plenty of time for reading for pleasure, reading as research, and writing my thesis. And lunch with Angelo, Gabeba, Kim, and Maura every day. Sometimes with Drew and Colette too.

I am also a Rape Crisis counsellor. I am dedicated to this work, and find nothing more rewarding than seeing a woman or girl move from despair in the first counselling session to telling me in later sessions how her life has started returning to her. It can take years to fully return, long after our sessions are over. It may never fully return. Not all clients keep coming back, but I have taught myself to stop wondering too hard. Instead, I hold on to the gratitude I feel for being able to do this work. Ingrid, Ayanda, and I are the odd ones out. Most other volunteers seem to be either psychologists or lawyers in training. Maybe it just seems that way.

One of the almost-lawyers asks me if I think there are too many lesbians at Rape Crisis Observatory. She is always asking bizarre questions or saying things like this; I don't always know how to answer her. This time I say no, there are probably just about enough lesbians. I don't know what to make of her question. I like women who ask bizarre questions.

And Rape Crisis is full of very strange, feminist women, many of whom are lesbians, including the odd inquisitor I don't always know how to talk to. I love it here because it is just the right mix of uncomfortable and wonderful.

Wonderful Penny. Dear Bronwyn.

Many weird feminists walking in and out. You'd think we would all be miserable, considering why we come here. We are not all friends. It's not that kind of community.

One weekend, one of the women friends that my boyfriend, Makanjila, and I go clubbing with, is pulled into a car on Sea Point Main Road, a few blocks away from our club.

For the next week, everybody in the group tries to convince her to go to Rape Crisis except me. Give her time, I plead. But she needs to go, they argue. I get it. But stop applying pressure. Stop doing all the well-intentioned, wrong things. None of the many stories of the survivors I counsel, or those of survivor friends, make it to my nightmares. I must be good at compartmentalising.

My obsessive fear of being abducted and gang-raped as a teenager has been replaced by this new fear of waking up like the woman in the flat in Gardens. My friend has just been kidnapped and raped while walking on a road I frequent, but the old abduction-gang-rape nightmare fear does not return.

I am only afraid of a man climbing through a window while I sleep in my flat alone. In the house we share, my bedroom window faces the street, but my fear is very specific. I know every single statistic on gender-based violence in South Africa, so I am well aware of my vulnerability, but I still walk where I want to when I want to. I know no woman is ever safe, and I may not win, but I will fight with all my might. And I am fighting when I insist on going where I want.

*Bloemfontein, 1997-2005*

I have moved here to the centre of the country to start my first adult job, and launch my career. Nothing will get between me and my carefully planned path to full professorship by the determined age in my life plan. Helene is a delight. She has a similar determined plan. We are so alike, even though it makes no sense how. Our department has several lovely people, and one truly vile one. My friends – Chijioke, Helene, and Mariza – would say two.

When I start working in this city, I am delighted to finally be making just enough money to afford to live alone. Patsy insists that

I buy a studio flat when I can't find a decent one in a block of flats to rent; our university has a staff subsidy.

Patsy always gives wonderful advice. I am not the kind of woman who always takes advice. I'm tired of looking, and we both know the unavailability has everything to do with the fact that I am Black. There are beautiful town houses available in a different part of town. But I am not interested in a town house, only my own flat. So, she finds an advert for a flat for sale; it is a north-facing studio flat, and I couldn't be happier. It is on the twentieth floor of a building. I often think about the woman in the Gardens flat, and I wish I still talked to my friend, but we have lost touch.

When I buy a bigger flat on the sixteenth floor of the same building, the only building in the city high enough for these numbers, I continue thinking about that woman from Gardens whose name I do not know. But I know nobody is climbing through my window. Not even the stalker, who campus security knows never to let back on campus, let alone near my office again.

This is a strange development. The arrival of my twenties meant that I was finally relieved that I was too old to be the candidate for public abduction. I had been unprepared to replace it with a new age-specific rape fear of rapists climbing through windows. I know the feminist literature tells us that most women are raped by men they know. That may well be. But where I live, this is small consolation and not entirely believable.

*East London, 2020*

I have not lived in a flat since I left Bloemfontein, which had changed its name to Mangaung by the time I left in August 2005. These days when I think about the woman in the Gardens flat, I send her positive energy and hope she feels it.

I know feminism has saved my life more times than I can remember. Feminist love is political. And I still feed my red-hot rage against patriarchy.

# ACKNOWLEDGEMENTS

Writing a book during a pandemic was not one of my best ideas. Through it all, I have had the most remarkable people cheering me on, challenging my ideas and listening to me discuss aspects of this book.

Melinda Ferguson, you have been a wonder through it all. Bibi Bakare-Yusuf, I cannot thank you enough for your multifaceted commitment to this project and your unwavering generosity. Your feedback and constant prompting and support have meant everything. Much appreciation also goes to the CRP team, with special thanks to Niki Igbaroola.

Angelo Fick, Helene Strauss, Danielle Bowler, Danai Mupotsa, Babalwa Magoqwana, Barbara Boswell, Grace Musila, Lynda Gichanda Spencer, Seehaam Samaai, Mamadi Matlhako, Gail Smith, Achieng Ojwang – you have all helped me refine many ideas in this book and inspired me through your own stellar work.

Yethu and Mamam, I could not have completed it without your support, including enduring my increased absent-mindedness as I wrote during the hard lockdown. Lebo, you are the most patient older sister for putting up with my forgetfulness as I wrote. Vuyani, thank you for listening to me talk about a single idea for hours at a time.

# NOTES

1. Gunn Allen, Paula, "Introduction," *Spider woman's granddaughters,* p. 8.
2. Alubo, Ogoh, "The public space in Nigeria," p. 77.
3. McKinnon, Catharine, *Sexual harassment of working women*, p. 95.
4. Horn, Jessica, "Re-righting the sexual body," p.8.
5. Mernissi, Fatema, "The meaning of spatial boundaries," p.350.
6. Fraser, Nancy, "Rethinking the public sphere," p. 79.
7. Mistry, Jyoti and Antje Schuhmann, "Introduction," *Gaze Regimes*, p. xvii.
8. Said, Edward, "Introduction," *Culture and Imperialism*, p. xiii,
9. Lerner, Gerda, *The Creation of Patriarchy*, p. 21.
10. Milani, Tommaso, "Querying the queer from Africa," p.75.
11. Bakare-Yusuf, Bibi, "Beyond determinism," p. 8.
12. Bakare-Yusuf, Bibi, "Beyond determinism," p. 8.
13. Walker, Alice, "Preface," *In search of our mother's gardens*
14. Mistry and Schuhmann, *Gaze Regimes*, p. xvi.
15. Robin, Corey, *Fear*, p. 3.
16. Robin, Corey, *Fear*, p. 18.
17. Jarymowicz, Maria and Daniel Bar-Tal, "The dominance of fear over hope", p.368.
18. Jarymowicz and Bar Tal, "The dominance of fear over hope," p. 369.
19. Jarymowicz and Bar Tal, "The dominance of fear over hope." p. 374-5.
20. Salzinger, Leslie, *Genders in production*, p. 2.
21. Pollard, Sidney, "Factory discipline in the industrial revolution," p. 254.
22. Salzinger, Leslie, *Genders in production*, p.13.
23. Salzinger, Leslie, *Genders in production*, p.13.

24. Pollard, Sidney, "Factory discipline in the industrial revolution," p. 254.
25. Youfsazai, Malala, "Death did not want to kill me," https://abcnews.go.com/International/malala-yousafzai-death-kill/story?id=20489800
26. Paul, Caroline, "Why do we teach girls that it's cute to be scared?" https://www.nytimes.com/2016/02/21/opinion/sunday/whydo-we-teach-girls-that-its-cute-to-be-scared.html
27. Frassinelli, Pier Paolo, *Borders, media crossings and the politics of translation*, p. 5.
28. Chambers, Maxine, "What do we mean by fluency?" p. 535.
29. Pikulski, John and David Chard, "Fluency," p. 510
30. Pikulski and Chard, "Fluency," p. 511.
31. Wright, Jennifer, "Women are afraid men will murder them," https://www.harpersbazaar.com/culture/politics/a15300130/sexual-consent-versus-coercion-aziz-ansari/
32. Wright, Jennifer, "Women are afraid men will murder them" https://www.harpersbazaar.com/culture/politics/a15300130/sexual-consent-versus-coercion-aziz-ansari/
33. O'Neal, Elizabeth, Jodie Plummert, and Carole Peterson, "Parent-child injury prevention conversations," p. 257.
34. Paul, Caroline, "Why do we teach girls that it's cute to be scared?"https://www.nytimes.com/2016/02/21/opinion/sunday/whydo-we-teach-girls-that-its-cute-to-be-scared.html
35. Morrongiello, Barbara and Theresa Dawber, "Parental influences," p. 227.
36. O'Neal, Plummert and Peterson, "Parent-child injury prevention conversations," p. 257.
37. O'Neal, Plummert and Peterson, "Parent-child injury prevention conversations," p. 262.
38. Eltahawy, Mona, *Seven necessary sins,* p. 140.
39. Smith, Misogynies, p. xvii.
40. Nyong'o, Lupita, "Speaking about Harvey Weinstein," https://www.nytimes.com/2017/10/19/opinion/lupita-nyongo-harvey-weinstein.html

41. Nyong'o, Lupita, "Speaking about Harvey Weinstein," https://www.nytimes.com/2017/10/19/opinion/lupita-nyongo-harvey-weinstein.html
42. Nyong'o, Lupita, "Speaking about Harvey Weinstein," https://www.nytimes.com/2017/10/19/opinion/lupita-nyongo-harvey-weinstein.html
43. Nyong'o, Lupita, "Speaking about Harvey Weinstein," https://www.nytimes.com/2017/10/19/opinion/lupita-nyongo-harvey-weinstein.html
44. Nyong'o, Lupita, "Speaking about Harvey Weinstein," https://www.nytimes.com/2017/10/19/opinion/lupita-nyongo-harvey-weinstein.html
45. Nyong'o, Lupita, "Speaking about Harvey Weinstein," https://www.nytimes.com/2017/10/19/opinion/lupita-nyongo-harvey-weinstein.html
46. Nyong'o, Lupita, "Speaking about Harvey Weinstein," https://www.nytimes.com/2017/10/19/opinion/lupita-nyongo-harvey-weinstein.html
47. Nyong'o, Lupita, "Speaking about Harvey Weinstein," https://www.nytimes.com/2017/10/19/opinion/lupita-nyongo-harvey-weinstein.html
48. Tamale, Sylvia, *African sexualities*, p.3.
49. Tamale, Sylvia, *African sexualities*, p.5.
50. Tamale, Sylvia, *African sexualities*, p. 5.
51. Castro, Laura Rodriguez, *Decolonial feminism*, p. 3.
52. Macharia, Keguro, "On Being Area-Studied," p. 185.
53. Wright, Jennifer, "Women are afraid men will murder them," https://www.harpersbazaar.com/culture/politics/a15300130/sexual-consent-versus-coercion-aziz-ansari/
54. Hayek, "Harvey Weinstein was my monster too," https://www.nytimes.com/interactive/2017/12/13/opinion/contributors/salma-hayek-harvey-weinstein.html
55. Kaur, Raminder "Mediating rape," p. 945.
56. Kaur, Raminder "Mediating rape," p. 949.

57. Talwar, Rajesh, *Courting injustice*, p. 4.
58. Talwar, Rajesh, *Courting injustice,* Preface.
59. Talwar, Rajesh, *Courting injustice*, Preface.
60. Ahmed, Saifuddin, Kokil Jaidka, and Jaeho Cho, "Tweeting India's Nirbhaya protest," p. 3.
61. Rajaram, Sneha, "Why do we continue to call her Nirbhaya?" https://www.firstpost.com/india/why-do-we-continue-to-call-her-nirbhaya-whats-wrong-with-saying-jyoti-singh-pandey-2550382.html
62. Susan, Nisha, "The trouble with being a goddess," http://theladiesfinger.com/the-trouble-with-being-a-goddess/
63. Rajaram, Sneha, "Why do we continue to call her Nirbhaya?" https://www.firstpost.com/india/why-do-we-continue-to-call-her-nirbhaya-whats-wrong-with-saying-jyoti-singh-pandey-2550382.html
64. Moeti, Koketso. (2020, 6 May). "South African women live with the constant burden"https://mg.co.za/article/2020-05-06-south-africanwomen-live-with-the-burden-of-constant-vigilance/
65. Govender, Pregs. "Strike a woman, strike a rock," p. 5.
66. Smith, Gail, "Survivors of sexual violence lift the lid," p. 27.
67. State vs Botha CC96/2019 ZAWCHC. As presiding justice, Judge Gayaat Salie-Hlophe of the Western Cape High Court declared that Luyanda Botha's lawyer and the prosecutor had come to a 'conviction and sentencing agreement' in accordance with 'justice,' before sentencing him to three life sentences, with a 25-year fixed non-parole agreement. See here for live coverage of the judgement: https://www.youtube.com/watch?v=BGpYdwznwjM, here: https://www.youtube.com/watch?v=R9obAd9tONQ, and here: https://www.youtube.com/watch?v=jYpOBkMZtco. Luyanda Botha's statements during court were widely reported in the media. See, among others, Nombembe, Philani. (2019, 6 November). "In his own words: Luyanda Botha: This is how I killed Uyinene," *Sowetan*, archived here: https://www.sowetanlive.co.za/news/south-africa/2019-

11-16-in-his-own-words-luyanda-botha-this-is-how-i-killed-uyinene/; Staff Reporter (2019, 18 November). "Uyinene killer: I intended to rape and kill," *Daily Voice*, archived here: https://www.dailyvoice.co.za/news/uyinene-killer-i-intended-to-rape-and-kill-37402346; Nkanjeni, Unathi. (2019, 09 September). "Five shocking revelations in Uyinene Mrwetyana's murder case," *Sunday Times*, archived here: https://www.timeslive.co.za/news/south-africa/2019-09-09-five-shocking-revelations-in-uyinene-mrwetyanas-murder-case/

68. As per note 67.
69. Pain, Rachel, "Space, sexual violence and social control," p. 415.
70. Smith, Joan, *Misogynies*, p, xv.
71. Smith, Joan, *Misogynies*, p. xv
72. Smith, Gail, "Fetching Saartjie," https://mg.co.za/article/2002-05-17-00-fetching-saartjie/
73. Smith, Gail, "Fetching Saartje," https://mg.co.za/article/2002-05-17-00-fetching-saartjie/
74. Antwi, Phanuel, Sarah Brophy, Helene Strauss and Y-Dang Troeung. "Postcolonial intimacies," p. 8.
75. Toyi-toyi is the South African combination of specific body movements performed in protest settings and/or marches with specific protest songs and slogans. Popularised by youth in the 1970s, it involves energetic movement of the body in different postures that may look like part-dance, part-jog, part-shooting, in some contexts; it also covers the performance of these movements by large collectives covering many kilometres rather than walking in a 'march.'
76. Tamale, Sylvia, *African Sexualities*, p. 5.
77. Lorde, Audre, *The Cancer Journals*, p. 15.
78. Siopis, Penny, *Shame*, p. 8.
79. Msimang, Sisonke, "Homesick," p. 27-30.
80. Msimang, Sisonke, "Homesick," p. 27.
81. Mohamed, Kharnita, "Remaking the ordinary," p. 33.
82. Mohamed, Kharnita, "Remaking the ordinary," p. 35.

83. Msimang, Sisonke, "Homesick," p. 28.
84. Frassinelli, Pier Paolo, p. 10.
85. Phadke, Shilpa, "Dangerous Liaisons," p. 1516.
86. Phadke, Shilpa, *Why Loiter?* p. 60.

# BIBLIOGRAPHY

Abonga, F., Kerali, R., Porter, H. E., & Tapscott, R. (2012). The power of naked protest in a shrinking democratic space. *Africa at LSE*, eprints.lse.ac.uk/1035556/I/the_power_of_naked_protest_africa_at_LSE.pdf

Abrahams, Y. (1997). The great long national insult: "Science," sexuality, sexuality and the Khoisan in the 18th and early 19th century. *Agenda: Empowering women for gender equity*, (13), 38-48.

Agence-France-Presse in New Delhi. (2018, July 11). Indian politician charged with rape of girl who tried to set herself alight. *The Guardian*. https://www.theguardian.com/world/2018/jul/11/indian-politician-charged-with-teenagers

Ahmed, S., Jaidka, K., & Cho, J. (2016). Tweeting India's Nirbhaya protest: A study of emotional dynamics in an online social movement. *Social Movement Studies, 16*(4), 447-465.

Allen, P. G. (1989). Introduction. In P. G. Allen (Ed.), *Spider Woman's granddaughters: Traditional tales and contemporary writing by Native American women* (pp. 1-30). Women's Press.

Alfino, M. (1991). Another look at the Derrida-Searle debate. *Philosophy & Rhetoric*. 24(2), 143-152.

Alubo, O. (2011). The public space in Nigeria: Politics of power, gender and exclusion. *Africa Development, 36*(1), 75-95.

Amadiume. I. (1987). *Male Daughters, Female Husbands: Gender and Sex in an African Society*. Zed Books.

Antwi, P., Brophy, S., Strauss, H., & Troeung, Y. (2013). Postcolonial intimacies: Gatherings, disruptions, departures. *Interventions, 15*(1), 1-9.

Anzaldua. G. (1987). *Borderlands/La Frontera: the new mestiza.* Aunt Lute.

Arondekar, A. (2012). Loitering as a feminist right. *Gender Studies,* 28.

Austin, J. L. (1962). *How to do things with words.* Oxford University Press.

Bakare-Yusuf, B. (2003). Beyond Determinism: The Phenomenology of *African Female Existence in Feminist Africa,* Issue 2, 2003.

Bennett, J. (2006). Rejecting roses: Introductory notes on pedagogies and sexualities. *Agenda: Empowering Women for Gender Equity,* (67), 68-79.

Bennett, J. (1997). 'Credibility, plausibility and autobiographical oral narrative: Some suggestions from the analysis of a rape survivor's testimony. In A. Levett, A. Kottler, E. Burman, & I. Parker (Eds.), *Culture, power and difference: Discourse analysis in South Africa* (pp. 96-108). University of Cape Town Press.

Bezuidenhout, N. (2013, October 11). Kana's rape confession shocks mother. *Cape Argus.* https://www.iol.co.za/news/kanas-rape-confession-shocks-mother-1590464

Bhana, D. (2012). Girls are not free – In and out of the South African school. *International Journal of Education Development,* *32*(2), 352-358.

Bhengu, C. (2019, October 18). Drugs, apologies and a life sentence: five chilling moments from Nicholas Ninow's court appearance. *Sowetan.* https://www.sowetanlive.co.za/news/south-africa/2019-10-18-drugs-apologies-a-life-sentence-five-chilling-moments-from-nicholas-ninows-court-appearance/

Bhongo, J. (2019, September 01). 'Baby Lee' killing: witness tells all. *Daily Dispatch.* https://www.dispatchlive.co.za/news/2019-09-01-baby-lee-killing-witness-tells-all/

Boswell, B. (2020). *And Wrote My Story Anyway: Black South African Women's Novels as Feminism.* Wits University Press

Brodie, Nechama. 2020. *Femicide in South Africa*. Kwela.

Camminga, B. (2018). "Gender refugees" in South Africa: The "common-sense" paradox. *African Spectrum*, *53*(1), 89-112.

Camminga, B. (2019). *Transgender refugees and the imagined South Africa: Bodies over borders and borders over bodies*. Palgrave MacMillan.

Castro, L. R. (2021). *Decolonial feminisms, power and place: Sentipensando with Rural Women in Colombia*. Palgrave MacMillan.

Chambers, F. (1997). What do we mean by fluency? *System*, *25(*4), 535-544.

Davids, N. (2013, February 08). Hunt on for more Bredasdorp suspects. *Sowetan*, https://www.sowetanlive.co.za/news/2013-02-08-hunt-on-for-more-bredasdorp-suspects/

Dayimani, M., Zifo, M. & Fuzile, B. (2019, August 31). SA world champion fighter shot dead by her police officer boyfriend. *Daily Dispatch*. https://www.timeslive.co.za/news/south-africa/2019-08-31-sa-world-champion-fighter-shot-dead-by-her-police-officer-boyfriend/

Derrida, J. (1967). *Of Grammatology*. (G. C. Spivak, Trans.). Johns Hopkins Press.

Derrida, J. (1988). *Limited Inc*. Northwestern University Press.

Diabate, N. (2016). Women's naked protest in Africa: comparative literature and its futures. In S. Puri & D. Castillo (Eds.), *Theorizing fieldwork in the humanities* (pp. 51-71). Palgrave MacMillan.

Driver, D. (1996). Drum Magazine (1951-99) and the spatial configurations of gender. In K. Darian-Smith, L. Gunner, & S. Nuttall (Eds.), *Text, theory, space: Land, literature and history in South Africa and Australia* (pp. 227-238). Routledge.

Dube, S. (2015). The faces of "swag" in South African reality television: Representations of "black" youth masculinities in *Running with the reps* [Master's thesis]. University of the Witwatersrand.

Du Bois, W. E. B. (1903). *The Souls of Black Folk: Essays and Sketches.* A. M. McClurg & Co.

Du Plessis, I. (2011). Nation, family and intimacy: the domain of the domestic in the social imaginary. *South African Review of Sociology*, *42*(2), 45-65.

Ebila, F., & Tripp, A. M. (2017). Naked transgressions: gendered symbolism in Ugandan land protests. *Politics, Groups and Identities, 51*, 25-45.

Egbunike, N. (2020, January 22). Another #SexForGrades scandal – and the birth of a movement against sexual harassment in Nigeria. *Global Voices.* https://globalvoices.org/2020/01/22/another-sexforgrades-scandal-and-the-birth-of-a-movement-against-sexual-harassment-in-nigeria/

Eltahawy, M. (2019). *The seven necessary sins for women and girls.* Beacon.

Evans, B. (2006). "I'd feel ashamed": Girls' bodies and sport. *Gender, Place and Culture*, *13*(5), 547-561.

Faith, K. (1993). *Unruly women: The politics of confinement and resistance.* Seven Stories Press.

Faludi, S. (1992). *Backlash: The undeclared war against women.* Crown Publishing.

Fasselt, R. (2014). "I'm not an Afropolitan – I'm of the continent": A conversation with Yewande Omotoso. *The Journal of Commonwealth Literature*, 1-6.

Fatunde, T. (2019, January 11). Mixed responses to jail time for "scapegoat" professor. *University World News.*

Felski, R. (1989). *Beyond feminist aesthetics.* Harvard University Press.

Ferguson, M. (2020). Wounded healers. In M. Ferguson (Ed.), *The lockdown collection* (pp. 10-16). Melinda Ferguson Books.

Fester, G. (2006). Some preliminary thoughts on sexuality, citizenship and constitutions: Are rights enough? *Agenda: Empowering women for gender equity*, (67), 100-111.

Filmmakers Against Racism (FAR) (2008). *FAR at DIFF*. http://filmmakers-against-racism.blogspot.co.za

Fraser, N. (1990). Rethinking the public sphere: A contribution to the critique of actually existing democracy. *Social Text, 25-26*, 56-80.

Fraser, N. (1989). *Unruly practices: Power, discourse and gender in contemporary social theory.* University of Minnesota Press.

Frassinelli, P. P. (2020). *Borders, media crossing and the politics of translation: The gaze from southern Africa.* Routledge.

Germaner, S. (2015, May 18). Hewitt sentenced to six years in jail. *The Star. https://www.iol.co.za/news/south-africa/gauteng/hewitt-sentenced-to-6-years-in-jail-1859971.*

Goldschmidt, S. (2014). *The hormone factory.* (H. Velmans, Trans.). Other Press.

Govender, P. (2006, March). Strike a woman, strike a rock. *Mail & Guardian*, 5.

Gqola, P. D. (2016). A peculiar place for a feminist? The new South African woman, *True Love* magazine and Lebo(gang) Mashile. *Safundi: The Journal of South African and American Studies, 17*(2), 119-136.

Gqola, P. D. (2007). How the "cult of femininity" and violent masculinities support endemic gender-based violence in South Africa. *African Identities, 5*(1), 111-124.

Gqola, P. D. (2008). In the clarity of a third-class compartment. In H. Habila and K. Sesay (Eds.), *Dreams, miracles and all that jazz: New adventures in African writing* (pp. 1-26). Picador Africa.

Gqola, P. D. (2013). The new South African woman. In *A renegade called Simphiwe.* Melinda Ferguson Books.

Gqola, P. D. (2015). *Rape: A South African nightmare.* Melinda Ferguson Books.

Gqola, P. D. (2017). *Reflecting rogue: Inside the mind of a feminist.* Melinda Ferguson Books.

Gray, C. (1998). Cultivating citizenship through xenophobia in Gabon, 1960-1995. *Africa Today*, *45*(3-4), 389-409.

Green, R. (Director). (2008). *Asikhulume* [Film]. Richard Green and Associates.

Gullone, E. (2000). The development of normal fear: A century of research. *Clinical Psychology Review*, *20*(4), 429-451.

Habermas, J. (1962). *The structural transformation of the public sphere: An inquiry into a category of bourgeois society.* (T. Burger & F. Lawrence, Trans.). MIT Press.

Hall, S. (1996). Introduction: Who needs identity? In S. Hall & P. du Gray (Eds.), *Questions of cultural identity* (pp. 1-17). Sage.

Hassim, S. (2006). *Women's organisations and democracy in South Africa: Contesting authority*. Wisconsin University Press.

Hassim, S. (2007). *Daughters are diamonds.* Reach Publishers.

Hassim, S. (2009a). After apartheid: Consensus, contention, and gender in South Africa's public sphere. *International Journal of Politics, Culture and Society*, *22*(4), 453-464.

Hassim, S. (2009b). Democracy's shadows: Sexual rights and gender politics in the rape trial of Jacob Zuma. *African Studies*, *68*(1), 57-77.

Hassim, S., Kupe, T., & Worby, E. (Eds.). (2008). *Go home or die here.* Wits University Press.

Hayek, S. (2017, December 12). Harvey Weinstein is my monster too. *New York Times.* https://www.nytimes.com/interactive/2017/12/13/opinion/contributors/salma-hayek-harvey-weinstein.html

hooks, b. (1984). *Feminist theory: from margin to centre.* South End.

Hooks, b. (1993). *Sisters of the yam: Black women and self-recovery.* South End.

Hooks, b. (1999). *Yearning: race, gender and cultural politics*. South End.

Hudson, R. F., Pullen, P. C., Lane, H. B., & Torgesen, J. (2008). The complex nature of reading fluency: A multidimensional view. *Reading and Writing Quarterly, 25*(1), 4-23.

Inchley, M. (2015). Theatre as advocacy: Asking for it and the audibility of women in Nirbhaya: The fearless one. *Theatre Research International, 40*(3), 272-282.

James, K., & Embrey, L. (2011). "Anyone could be lurking around!": Constraints on adolescent girls' recreational activities after dark. *World Leisure Journal, 43*(4), 44-52.

Jarymowicz, M., & Bar-Tal, D. (2006). The dominance of fear over hope in the life of individuals and collectives. *European Journal of Social Psychology, 36*, 367-392.

Jordaan, N. (2019, September 16). Watch: Rapist Nicholas Ninow also guilty of defeating ends of justice and drug possession. *Dispatch Live*. https://www.sowetanlive.co.za/news/south-africa/2019-10-18-drugs-apologies-a-life-sentence-five-chilling-moments-from-nicholas-ninows-court-appearance/

Jordaan, N. (2019, September 19). Dros 'rapist' case: waitress quit job because she can't forget 'the blood, the screaming'. *Herald Live*. https://www.heraldlive.co.za/news/2019-09-16-dros-rapist-case-waitress-quit-job-because-she-cant-forget-the-blood-the-screaming/

Jordaan, N. (2019, September 02). Theology student and her grandfather found murdered at home. https://www.timeslive.co.za/news/south-africa/2019-09-02-theology-student-and-her-grandfather-found-murdered-at-home/

Kaur, R. (2017). Mediating rape: The "Nirbhaya effect" in the creative and digital arts. *Signs, 42*(4), 945-976.

Knight, T. (2019, November 20). Two in court for murder of Jesse Hess and grandfather. *Daily Maverick*. https://www.

dailymaverick.co.za/article/2019-11-20-two-in-court-for-murder-of-jesse-hess-and-grandfather/

Lerner, G. (1987). *The creation of patriarchy.* Oxford University Press.

Lewis, D. (2005). African gender research and postcoloniality: Legacies and challenges. In O. Oyewumi (Ed.), *African gender studies: A reader* (pp. 381-396). Palgrave MacMillan.

Lewis, D. (2001). Introduction: African feminisms. *Agenda: Empowering Women for Gender Equity,* (50), 4-10.

Ligaga, D. (2017). Thinking around genre: The moral narrative and femininity in Kenyan popular media. *The Cambridge Journal of Postcolonial Literary Inquiry, 4*(2), 222-236.

Lloyd, G. (1984). *The man of reason: "Male" and "female" in Western philosophy.* Routledge.

Lorde, A. (1997). *The cancer journals.* Aunt Lute.

Lovera, P. S. (2020, February 13). *El Salvador: The story of Karla Turcios.* BBC. https://www.bbc.co.uk/programmes/w3csy5dv

Luckoff, P. (2019, November 13). Aunt of slain student Jesse Hess confirms murder suspect is close family member. *Cape Talk.* https://www.capetalk.co.za/articles/366823/aunt-of-slain-student-jesse-hess-confirms-murder-suspect-is-close-family-member

MacKinnon, C. (1979). *Sexual harassment of working women: A case of sex discrimination.* Yale University Press.

Macharia, K. (2016). On being area-studied: A litany of complaint. *GLQ: Journal of Lesbian and Gay Studies, 22*(2), 183-190.

Macharia, K. (2018, September 19). On quitting. *New Inquiry.* https://thenewinquiry.com/on-quitting/

Macharia, K. (2009). Queering African studies. *Criticism, 51*(1) https://digitalcommons.wayne.edu/criticism/vol51/iss1/7

Madriz, E. (1997). *Nothing bad happens to good girls: Fear of crime in women's lives.* California University Press.

Magubane, Z. (2001). Which bodies matter? Feminist poststructuralism, race, and the curious theoretical odyssey of the Hottentot Venus. *Gender and Society, 15*(6), 816-834.

Magubane, Z. (2003). *Bringing the empire home: Race, class, and gender in Britain and colonial South Africa.* University of Chicago Press.

Maregele, B. (2013, October 14). Anene 'drunk and dancing' at pub, testifies close friend. *Cape Times.* https://www.pressreader.com/south-africa/cape-times/20131014/281767036949563

Masina, N. (2011). Black like me: Representations of Black women in advertisements placed in contemporary South African magazines [Master's thesis]. University of the Witwatersrand.

Matambamadzo, I. (2006). Terrified by the Voice of the People. *Rhodes Journalism Review.* 26(September), 41-42.

Mbao, W. (2009). Imagined pasts, suspended presents: South Africa's literature in the contemporary moment [Doctoral thesis]. Stellenbosch University.

McCool, A. (2020, March 19). "After prison, I'm stronger, more vulgar!": The irrepressible Stella Nyanzi. *The Guardian,* https://www.theguardian.com/books/2020/mar/19/prison-irrepressible-stella-nyanzi-uganda-poet

Mehta, D. (2016). *Autonomy of violence* [Film]. Hamilton Mehta Productions.

Mernissi, F. (2015). The meaning of spatial boundaries. In S. Bordo, M. C. Alcalde, & E. Rosenman (Eds.), *Provocations: A transnational reader in the history of feminist thought* (pp. 350-362). University of California Press.

Meintjes, S. (1994, July). *Women's naked protest, Dobsonville, 1990: Gender consciousness and the body politic* [Seminar paper]. Wits History Workshop, University of the Witwatersrand.

Meyer, D. (2019, September 02). Missing UCT student Uyinene Mrwetyana was 'bludgeoned with a scale' at post office. *Times Live.* https://www.timeslive.co.za/news/south-africa/2019-09-

02-breaking-missing-uct-student-was-bludgeoned-with-a-scale-in-post-office/

Milani, T. (2014). Querying the queer from Africa: Precarious bodies, precarious gender. *Agenda: Empowering Women for Gender Equity,* (28), 75-85.

Mistry, J., & Schumann, A. (Eds.). (2015). *Gaze regimes: Film and feminisms in Africa.* Wits University Press.

Mitchell, C., de Lange, N., & Moletsane, R. (2017). Addressing sexual violence in South Africa: "Gender activism in the making." In E. Oinas, H. Onodera & L. Surpää (Eds.), *What politics? Youth and political engagement in Africa* (pp.317-336). Brill.

Misejewski, L. (2007). Queen Latifah, unruly women, and the bodies of romantic comedy. *Genders, 46.* https://cdn.atria.nl/ezines/IAV_606661_2021_51/g46_mizejewski.html

Mitchley, A. (2020, March 06). Dros rapist Nicholas Ninow asks for leave to appeal, says rape was not premeditated. *News24.* https://www.news24.com/news24/SouthAfrica/News/exclusive-convicted-dros-rapist-nicholas-ninow-kept-in-a-single-cell-away-from-other-prisoners-20191011

Moeti, K. (2020, May 6). South African women live with the burden of "constant vigilance." *Mail & Guardian.* https://mg.co.za/article/2020-05-06-south-africanwomen-live-with-the-burden-of-constant-vigilance/

Moeti, K. (2020, January 22). What not to do when women cry for help. *City Press.* https://www.news24.com/citypress/voices/what-not-to-do-when-womencry-for-help-20200117

Mohamed, K. (2020). Remaking the ordinary. In M. Ferguson (Ed.), *The lockdown collection* (pp. 31-36). Melinda Ferguson Books.

Morais, S. (2019, September 02). Men who shot and killed boxing champion Leighandre Jegels dies in hospital. *News 24.* https://www.news24.com/news24/SouthAfrica/News/breaking-man-who-shot-and-killed-boxing-champion-leighandre-jegels-dies-in-hospital-20190902

Mordi, K. (2019, October 10). Nigeria: Sex for grades [Audio podcast episode]. In *The documentary podcast*. BBC. https://www.bbc.co.uk/sounds/play/w3csy5d3

Morrongiello, B. A., & Dawber, T. (1999). Parental influences on toddlers' injury-risk behaviour: Are sons and daughters socialised differently? *Journal of Applied Developmental Psychology*, *20*(2), 227-251.

Motsemme, N. (2004). "The mute always speak": On women's silences at the Truth and Reconciliation Commission. *Current Sociology*, *52*(5), 909-932.

Msimang, S. (2020). Homesick: Notes on lockdown. In M. Ferguson (Ed.), *The lockdown collection* (pp. 27-30). Melinda Ferguson Books.

Mulvey, L. (1975). Visual pleasure and narrative cinema. *Screen*. 16(3), 6-18.

Mulvey, L. (1989). *Visual and other pleasures*. Indiana University Press.

Mupotsa, D. (2014). White weddings [Doctoral thesis]. University of the Witwatersrand.

Mupotsa, D. (2015). The promise of happiness: Desire, attachment and freedom in post/apartheid South Africa. *Critical Arts*, *29*(2), 183-198.

Musila, G. A. (2017). Navigating epistemic disarticulations. *African Affairs*, *116*, 692-704.

Nagar, R. (2000). "I'd rather be rude than ruled": Gender, place and communal politics among South Asian communities in Dar es Salaam. *Women's Studies International Forum*,*23*(5), 575-581.

Ndamase, M. (2019, September 02). Leighandre 'Baby Lee' Jegels murder accused dies in hospital. *Sowetan*. https://www.sowetanlive.co.za/news/south-africa/2019-09-02-leighandre-baby-lee-jegels-murder-accused-dies-in-hospital/

Nyong'o, L. (2017, October 19). Speaking out about Harvey Weinstein. *New York Times.* https://www.nytimes.com/2017/10/19/opinion/lupita-nyongo-harveyweinstein.html

Ogidan, S. (2020, February 17). I am yet to receive my certificate after exposing randy lecturer, Osagie cries out. *Independent.* https://www.independent.ng/i-am-yet-to-receive-my-certificate-after-exposing-randy-lecturerosagie-cries-out/

O fm. (2012, October 16). Bob Hewitt removed from Hall of Fame after sex scandal. http://www.ofm.co.za/article/National/125923/Bob-Hewitt-removed-from-tennis-Hall-of-Fame-after-sex-scandal.

Ojenkule, A. (2019, July 10). Nigerians react to BBC exposé on African lecturers in #SexForGrades. *Pulse.* https://www.pulse.ng/bi/politics/nigerians-react-to-bbcexpose-on-african-lecturers-in-sexforgrades/dge2bs7

Okiror, S. (2020, February 21). Stella Nyanzi marks release from jail with Yoweri Museveni warning. *The Guardian.* https://www.theguardian.com/global-development/2020/feb/21/stella-nyanzi-marks-releasefrom-jail-in-uganda-with-yoweri-museveni-warning

Omer, R. (2017). The modern and the traditional: African women and colonial morality. *Inquiries: Social Sciences, Arts and Humanities,* 9(10) www.inquiriesjournal.com/articles/1655/the-modern-and-thetraditional-african-woman-and-colonial-morality

O'Neal, E. E., Plumert, J. M., & Peterson, C. (2016). Parent-child injury prevention conversations following a trip to the emergency department. *Journal of Pediatric Psychology, 41*(2), 256-264.

Oyeronke, O. (2005). Visualising the body: Western theories and African subjects. In O. Oyewumi (Ed.), *African gender studies: A reader* (pp. 3-22). Palgrave MacMillan.

Pain, R. (1991). Space, sexual violence and social control. *Progress in Human Geography*. 15(4), 415-431.

Paul, C. (2016, February 20). Why do we teach girls that it's cute to be scared? *New York Times*. https://www.nytimes.com/2016/02/21/opinion/sunday/whydo-we-teach-girls-that-its-cute-to-be-scared.html

Paulson, S., & Spivak, G. C. (2016, July 29). Critical intimacy: An interview with Gayatri Chakravorty Spivak. *LA Review of Books* https://lareviewofbooks.org/article/critical-intimacy-interview-gayatri-chakravorty-spivak

Phadke, S. (2007, April 20). Dangerous liaisons: Women and men: Risk and reputation in Mumbai. *Economic and Political Weekl.*, 1510-1518.

Phadke, S. (2020). Defending frivolous fun: Feminist acts of claiming public spaces in South Asia. *South Asia: Journal of South Asian Studies*, *43*(2), 281-293.

Phadke, S. (2005). "You can be lonely in a crowd": The production of safety in Mumbai. *Indian Journal of Gender Studies*, *12*(1), 41-62.

Pikulski, J. J., & Chard, D. J. (2005). Fluency: Bridge between decoding and reading comprehension. *The Reading Teacher*, *58*(6), 510-519.

Prince, M., & Ferguson, M. (1998). *The history of Mary Prince, a West Indian slave, as told by herself.* University of Michigan Press.

Potgieter, C. (2006). The imagined future for gays and lesbians in South Africa: Is this it? *Agenda: Empowering Women for Gender Equity*, (67), 4-8.

Radford, J., & Russel, D. E. H. (Eds). (1992). *Femicide: The Politics of Woman Killing*. Twayne.

Rajaram, S. (2015, December 18). Why do we continue to call her Nirbhaya? What's wrong with saying Jyoti Singh Pandey? *Firstpost.* https://www.firstpost.com/india/why-do-we-continue-to-call-her-nirbhaya-whats-wrong-withsaying-jyoti-singh-pandey-2550382.html

Rich, A. (1980). Compulsory heterosexuality and lesbian existence. *Signs, 5*(4), 631-660.

Riger, S., & Gordon, M. T. (1981). The fear of rape: A study in social control. *Journal of Social Issues, 37*(4), 71-92.

Robin, C. (2004). *Fear: The history of a political idea.* Oxford University Press.

Rowe, K. (1995). *The unruly woman: Gender and the genres of laughter.* University of Texas Press.

Ruhfus, J. (Director). (2018). *The murder of Marielle Franco* [Film]. AlJazeera. https://www.aljazeera.com/program/people-power/2019/6/6/the-murder-of-marielle-franco

Russell, D. E. H. (2011). 'Femicide': The Power of a Name. http://www.dianarussel.com/femicide_the_power_of_a_name.html.

Safi, M. (2018, April 11). Man who accused Indian politician of raping daughter dies in prison. *The Guardian.* https://www.theguardian.com/world/2018/apr/11/man-accused-india-politician-raping-daughter-dies-in-custody

Said, E. (1993) *Culture and imperialism.* Chatto & Windus.

Salmon, R., & Elata-Alster, G. (1992). Retracing a writerly text: In the footsteps of a Midrashic sequence on the creation of male and female. In A. Loades & M. McLain (Eds.), *Hermeneutics, the Bible and literary criticism* (pp. 177-197). Palgrave MacMillan.

Salo, E. (2007). Gendered citizenship, race and women's differentiated access to power in the new South Africa. *Agenda: Empowering Women for Gender Equity*, (72), 187-196.

Salo, E. (2005, March 23). *Gender-based violence and sexuality in South Africa.* [Conference proceeding]. Harold Wolpe Memorial Trust Open Dialogue Lecture. http://wolpetrust.org.za/dialogue2005/CT032005salo-achmat_transcript.pdf

Salzinger, L. (2003). *Genders in production: Making workers in Mexico's global factories.* University of California Press.

Scully, D., & Bart, P. (2003). A funny thing happened on the way to the orifice: Women in gynecology textbooks. *Feminism and Psychology*, *13*(1), 11-16.

Seacole, M., & Salih, S. (2005). *The wonderful adventures of Mrs Seacole in many lands.* Penguin Classics.

Sears, H. A., Byers, A., Whelan, J. J., & Saint-Pierre, M. (2006). "If it hurts you, then it's not a joke": Adolescent girls' and boys' use and experience of abusive behavior in dating relationships. *Journal of Interpersonal Violence*, 21(9), 1191-1207.

Searle, J. (1977). Reiterating the differences. *Glyph 2.* Johns Hopkins University Press.

Sharma, V. (2018, April 15). *The life of Brazil's Marielle Franco* [Video]. Now This Word. https://www.youtube.com/watch?v=72-QbwDnUQI

Siopis, P. (2016) *Shame.* Stevenson.

Sithole, X. (Director). (2001). *Shouting silent* [Film]. NayaNaya Productions.

Sithole, X. (Director). (2008). *Martine and Thandeka* [Film]. NayaNaya Productions.

Smith, G. (2002, May 12). Fetching Saartje. *Mail & Guardian*, https://mg.co.za/article/2002-05-17-00-fetching-saartjie/.

Smith, G. (2006, April). Survivors of sexual violence lift the lid on their ordeals. *City Press*, 27.

Spencer, L. G., Ligaga, L., & Musila, G. A. (2018). Gender and popular imaginaries in Africa. *Agenda: Empowering Women for Gender Equity,* (32), 3-9.

Spitz, A. (Director). (2008). *Angels on our shoulders* [Film]. Left-Eye Productions.

Spivak, G. C. (1988). Can the subaltern speak? In C. Nelson & L. Grossberg (Eds.), *Marxism and the interpretation of culture* (pp. 267-310). University of Illinois Press.

Stegeman, K. (2013, February 11). Remembering Anene Booysen: The sound, the fury and the politicking. *Mail & Guardian*. http://mg.co.za/article/2013-02-11-remembering-anene-booysen-the-sound-thefury-and-the-politicking

Strauss, H. (2011). Cinema of social recuperation: Xenophobic violence and migrant subjectivity in contemporary South Africa. *Subjectivity*, *4*, 103-20.

Summers, C. (2006). Radical rudeness: Ugandan social critiques in the 1940s. *Journal of Social History, 39*(3), 741-770.

Susan, N. (2013, September 10). The trouble with being a goddess. *The Ladies Finger.* http://theladiesfinger.com/the-trouble-with-being-a-goddess/

Tamale, S. (2011). Introduction. In S. Tamale (Ed.), *African sexualities: A reader* (pp.1-8). Pambazuka Press.

Talwar, R. (2013). *Courting injustice: The Nirbhaya case and its aftermath.* Hay House.

Tlali, M. (1988). *Footprints in the quag.* David Phillips.

Truth, S. 1851. Ain't I a Woman?, Women's Convention, Akron, Ohio. https://thehermitage.com/wp-content/uploads/2016/02/Sojourner-Truth_Aint-I-a-Woman_1851.pdf

Tyler, I., & Gill, R. (2013). Postcolonial girl. *Interventions*, *15*(1), 78-94.

Ussher, J. M. (2003). Biology as destiny: The legacy of Victorian gynecology in the 21st century. *Feminism and Psychology, 13*(1), 17-22.

Valentine, G. (1989). The geography of women's fear. *Area, 21*(4), 385-390.

Van Der Berg, C. (2019, September 08). Baby Lee: such a sad, tragic, violent loss. *Sunday Tribune*. https://www.iol.co.za/sport/opinion/baby-lee-such-a-sad-tragic-violent-loss-32553068

Vera, B. (1999) *Butterfly Burning*. Baobab.

Whitcraft, T., & Pearson, M. (2013). Malala Yousafzai: Death did not want to kill me. *ABC News.* https://abcnews.go.com/International/malala-yousafzai-death-kill/story?id=20489800

Win, E. (2020). Stigma and discrimination kill the soul. In M. Ferguson (Ed.), *The lockdown collection* (pp. 232-236). Melinda Ferguson Books.

Wright, J. (2018, January 17). Women are afraid men will kill them. *Harpers Bazaar.* https://www.harpersbazaar.com/culture/politics/a15300130/sexual-consent-versus-coercion-aziz-ansari/

Williams, H., & Williams J. (Directors). (2017). *Liar.* [TV Series]. Two Brothers Pictures.

Williams, R. (1977). *Marxism and Literature.* Oxford University Press

Yates, V. L. (2015). Biology is destiny: The deficiencies of women in Aristotle's biology and *Politics. Arethusa,* 48(1), 1-16.

# Support Female Fear Factory

**We hope you enjoyed reading this book. It was brought to you by Cassava Republic Press, an award-winning independent publisher based in Abuja and London. If you think more people should read this book, here's how you can support:**

1. **Recommend it.** Don't keep the enjoyment of this book to yourself; tell everyone you know. Spread the word to your friends and family.

2. **Review, review review**. Your opinion is powerful and a positive review from you can generate new sales. Spare a minute to leave a short review on Amazon, GoodReads, Wordery, our website and other book buying sites.

3. **Join the conversation.** Hearing somebody you trust talk about a book with passion and excitement is one of the most powerful ways to get people to engage with it. If you like this book, talk about it, Facebook it, Tweet it, Blog it, Instagram it. Take pictures of the book and quote or highlight from your favourite passage. You could even add a link so others know where to purchase the book from.

4. **Buy the book as gifts for others.** Buying a gift is a regular activity for most of us – birthdays, anniversaries, holidays, special days or just a nice present for a loved one for no reason... If you love this book and you think it might resonate with others, then please buy extra copies!

5. **Get your local bookshop or library to stock it.** Sometimes bookshops and libraries only order books that they have heard about. If you loved this book, why not ask your librarian or bookshop to order it in. If enough people request a title, the bookshop or library will take note and will order a few copies for their shelves.

6. **Recommend a book to your book club.** Persuade your book club to read this book and discuss what you enjoy about the book in the company of others. This is a wonderful way to share what you like and help to boost the sales and popularity of this book. You can also join our online book club on Facebook at Afri-Lit Club to discuss books by other African writers.

7. **Attend a book reading.** There are lots of opportunities to hear writers talk about their work. Support them by attending their book events. Get your friends, colleagues and families to a reading and show an author your support.

**Thank you!**

Stay up to date with the latest books, special offers and exclusive content with our monthly newsletter.
Sign up on our website:
www.cassavarepublic.biz

Twitter: @cassavarepublic
Instagram: @cassavarepublicpress
Facebook: facebook.com/CassavaRepublic
Hashtag: #FemaleFearFactory #ReadCassava

Transforming a manuscript into the book you're now reading is a team effort. Cassava Republic Press would like to thank everyone who helped in the production *Female Fear Factory*:

**Editorial**
Bibi Bakare-Yusuf
Ibukun Olowu
Layla Mohamed

**Design and Production**
Wendy Scott (Cover Designer)
Deepak Sharma (Layout Designer)

**Marketing, Sales & Publicity**
Kofo Okunola
Niki Igbaroola
Rhoda Nuhu

**Administration**
Adeyinka Adewole
Boluwatito Sanusi